Wellsprings of a Nation

WELLSPRINGS
OF A NATION

AMERICA BEFORE 1801

A bicentennial exhibition from
the collections of the
American Antiquarian Society
at the Worcester Art Museum
April 19–June 5, 1977

TEXT BY RODGER D. PARKER

American Antiquarian Society

WORCESTER · 1977

This exhibition and the lecture series accompanying it were made possible by a grant from the National Endowment for the Humanities, a Federal agency. Publication of the catalogue was aided by grants from the Endowment, the Massachusetts Council on the Arts and Humanities, and the Worcester Bicentennial Commission.

TABLE OF CONTENTS

FOREWORD

THE AMERICAN ANTIQUARIAN SOCIETY was founded in 1812 in order to advance the arts and sciences not only by collecting and preserving the materials which mark their progress and which tend to enlarge the sphere of human knowledge, but also by assisting the researches of future historians of our country that posterity might be improved and interested by the history of moral and political events.

The exhibition which is recorded in this catalogue is an effort in this latter day to present to the public some of the literary and artistic antiquities of the formative years of our nation. It constitutes the final public episode in the series of projects sponsored by the Society in honor of our nation's bicentennial anniversary. Other observances have included a film utilizing lithographic prints of the Jacksonian Period to illustrate American life and how Americans looked at themselves. The motion picture is entitled *Pictures to Serve the People: American Lithography, 1830–1855* and is available from the Museum of Modern Art. With the cooperation of and financial support from the American Newspaper Publishers Association Foundation, the Society published a series of sixty-four weekly newspaper articles which were written by Professor Francis G. Walett of Worcester State College. Each article was illustrated by documents drawn from the Society's collections. The series was published in nearly 200 newspapers. Later the articles were reprinted in book form under the title *Patriots, Loyalists and Printers: Bicentennial Articles on the American Revolution*. Also, Professor Walett and the Society's staff selected 135 documents from the collections which were reprinted in facsimile under the title *American Bicentennial Historical Facsimile Packet*. The set of reproductions, which is accompanied by a teacher's manual, is designed for secondary school stu-

dents and was published by Allyn & Bacon, Inc., textbook publishers of Boston. AAS staff members also selected a number of these facsimiles which were then mounted on panels and circulated to Worcester public schools as a bicentennial exhibition. The Society, in addition, sponsored or accommodated public lectures by four historians, Henry C. Borger, George A. Billias, Arthur F. Schrader, and William L. Joyce, speaking on aspects of the Revolution.

Lectures by Jack P. Greene of The Johns Hopkins University, William G. McLoughlin of Brown University, Robert E. Spiller of the University of Pennsylvania, and Wendell D. Garrett of *The Magazine Antiques* were scheduled to be held during the run of this exhibition to explicate certain aspects of the politics, religion, literature, and art, respectively, of the Revolutionary Era. The Society's final bicentennial contribution will be the publication of a book of scholarly essays, *The Press and the American Revolution*, edited by Bernard Bailyn and James Russell Wiggins.

The present exhibition has been organized by members of the staff of the Society, namely Georgia B. Bumgardner, John B. Hench, and William L. Joyce. The introduction, much of the selection of objects, and the text of the exhibition labels were written or performed by Rodger D. Parker.

An exhibition that features historical documents presents challenges different from those for exhibitions displaying the more usual art objects. These challenges were particularly interesting in the writing of this catalogue. The objective was to produce an exhibition and catalogue that carried an idea, or coherent interpretive theme, rather than to display several score of high spots documenting American history before 1801. Thus, the items exhibited here have been selected to serve as visual footnotes for Mr. Parker's introductory essay, which represents one historian's view of America's history during the Colonial, Revolutionary, and Federalist periods. That view is of the American people's efforts to be the model for the rest of the world to emulate. The Society hopes that the contents of the exhibition will improve and interest each viewer.

Staff members at the Worcester Art Museum have taken a keen interest in the successful organization and mounting of the exhibition. We are particularly grateful to the director, Richard Stuart Teitz, and to James A. Welu, the assistant curator of the collection, for close attention to detail and for the stunning arrangement of the objects in the exhibit. To all other staff members of the Society and the Museum who have played a part in this enterprise we express our appreciation.

The financing of the exhibition was defrayed through a generous grant from the National Endowment for the Humanities. We are grateful to Irene Burnham and Nancy Englander of the Division of Public Programs for their encouragement and support. Much of the cost of the publication of the catalogue was absorbed by the Endowment's grant and by two matching grants from the Worcester Bicentennial Commission and the Massachusetts Council on the Arts and Humanities. To these groups we tender our thanks.

M. A. McCorison
Director and Librarian

INTRODUCTION

'Thus in the beginning all the world was America.'—John Locke

THE IDEA OF AMERICA as Canaan, wherein man could be reborn, had been declared in England and Europe long before any settlements existed in the New World. This notion was reinforced by the often fanciful accounts of explorers and adventurers. Once the colonists arrived in the New World, moreover, this mythology was reinforced by the covenant theories of the Puritans, the stubborn optimism of the settlers, and an inherited belief in English superiority. As part of the belief in their own superiority and uniqueness, the Puritans felt that the society they established in America would ultimately be imitated by all of Europe. 'If we succeed,' asserted John Winthrop, the governor of the Massachusetts Bay Company, men would say of later plantations, 'the Lord make it like that of New England.' 'We shall be,' he prophesied, 'as a City upon a Hill, the eyes of all people are upon us.'

Cotton Mather, a third-generation Puritan, expressed this theme in his *Magnalia Christi Americana* by insisting that 'the Holy City . . . a City, the streets whereof will be Pure Gold,' would be found in America, and that the Puritans in New England were destined to populate that city. He further asserted in *Theopolis Americana* that the 'wonders of the Christian Religion' had fled 'from the Deprivations of Europe to the American Strand,' where the founders not only intended to save themselves, but redeem the world as well. New England, and eventually America as a whole, had something to teach all men by its example.

The Puritans believed that they had escaped from history, that they had been reborn, and that the fate of the world now rested with them. This belief acted as an extraordinary impetus to social thought, and their early writings constantly focused on the utopian nature of their undertaking, and on 'the new divide in the history of mankind' that Massachusetts represented. The Puritans believed that in this setting religious, social, and political truths would emerge. Church organization would follow God's word and by its success demand emulation. Social relationships among Christians would achieve a new brotherly quality. Theirs was an errand into the wilderness, an attempt to resurrect something that had long since been lost. It was a return to a simpler, purer Christian past, to God's original principles, and as such must be followed by the rest of mankind.

For the Pilgrims who came to America a decade before Winthrop's Puritans, mission meant separating themselves rather completely from the Old World. Before landing at Plymouth Rock in 1620, the Pilgrims had subscribed to the Mayflower Compact—an agreement to govern themselves by majority rule, independent of the corrupt and enervating church and state of England. Likewise, those Puritans who sailed with the charter of the Massachusetts Bay Company in 1630 resolved to make their charter the constitutional basis for a holy commonwealth which would be beyond the king's reach across the Atlantic, and which would serve as a beacon for the rest of mankind.

Others who came to the New World, including those who settled Virginia, also believed that they were a peculiar people, destined to live in a more perfect community than any known in the Old World. Although Virginians talked less than New Englanders about God's special endorsement, every settler knew that Englishmen had been serving His greater glory by removing to Virginia and by making the project successful. Stories had long circulated in England that heathen souls could be saved in Virginia and that the province was quite possibly a corner of heaven itself. Moreover, settlers themselves often referred to their newfound home as 'God's country,' and believed that other people would follow their example.

To be sure, the realities of daily existence in the earliest colonies belied the myth of America as Canaan. When confronted with survival in the wilderness, most settlers were disillusioned. The wilderness was so immense, lonely, and perilous that many simply gave up. Yet those who persevered found in their very agony and struggle proof of their own destiny and mission, and reinforcement for their view that they were God's chosen people. The settlers of New England, for example, not having found a land flowing with milk and honey, came to see the promised land as the very wilderness through which a generation was obliged to wander before entering Canaan. If they could not build their Zion themselves, then they could bestow it upon their children through their diligence, perseverence, and faith. Orientation toward the future rather than the past—the idea of working for one's posterity, for the children, so that their lives might be better than one's own—became deeply rooted in the American psyche.

In such a setting, with so many hardships to overcome, one's faith in one's own actions and beliefs had to be sustained at all costs. Having found the independence, whether spiritual or material, that they had sought, they could not allow that indepencence to be threatened. Accordingly, toleration was, especially in New England, a concept that few of them recognized or approved. What they wanted was freedom from interference by opposing religious sects or unfriendly authorities. Once firmly entrenched themselves, sects that had been persecuted in England became equally zealous to root out heretics from their own order. The New World facilitated their zealotry by affording so much space that those banished from any orthodoxy, or who chose to leave of their own accord, had every opportunity to set up their own particular community with its own orthodoxy.

Roger Williams was able in this way to establish in 1631 his own social order in Providence, and Puritans in Massachusetts Bay were spared the unsettling doctrines and presence of someone who interfered with their beliefs. Williams was so taken with the importance of individual liberty, in fact, that no formal church was organized until March 1639, when a group in Providence united in a fellowship which Baptists claim as the first of their denomination in the New World. Indeed, Williams expanded the notion of independence to mean 'freedom to' as well as 'freedom from.' Not only Baptists of various shades of belief, but also Jews, Quakers, and other sectarians lived and worshiped in Rhode Island as they pleased.

The New England congregationalists did not go quite so far as Williams, but they too made important changes in the political, religious, and social order. For example, no hierarchy ruled over the individual churches. Such hierarchies smacked of Roman Catholicism and had been abandoned. The congregational churches, moreover, in their attempt to return to original principles, had simplified ritual and made religion somewhat more comprehensible to the common man. There was an element of egalitarianism in the congregational way as well, for, before anyone could gain membership and receive the sacraments, no matter what his social position, he had to experience saving grace, and describe it clearly to the congregation. This equalization—whether in politics, social relations, or religion—would in time become an integral part of the American style. For the moment, it helped reinforce the colonists' notions of their special mission and place in the world.

The need to be part of a Divine Plan was closely connected with the colonists' need for order. In New England the churches had the responsibility of maintaining good order in the community as well as ensuring the proper behavior of its members. Any offender against society faced sanctions not only from a civil court, but from his church as well. Accordingly, both secular and religious institutions responded to deviant behavior swiftly and surely. Such response was based not only on the fact that order had to be maintained for the survival of the colony, but also because order was the will of God.

Throughout the seventeenth century church discipline gradually weakened; there were unmistakable forces of secularization at work. However, the erosion of church authority was slow. Many men, urged on by their ministers, still judged themselves by the rigorous standards of the first generation.

The churches recognized these changes and expanded their restricted membership somewhat in 1662. Puritan leaders formulated the Halfway Covenant, which permitted church admission for the children of those who had the intense 'converting experience' in the early days of settlement. Thus church benches could remain filled.

By yielding to secular values the New Englanders became swept up in a process that had long affected those who had settled in the South. To be sure, Dissenters, and even a few Catholics, had found their way to Virginia, but Anglicans dominated. During the seventeenth century, the House of Burgesses from time to time enacted laws aimed at Anglican conformity, but the landowners were eager for servants and settlers, and so nobody inquired too closely into the religion of a newcomer. Furthermore, the Episcopal ritual followed Low Church practice, for most Virginians detested ceremony, preferring instead demonstrations of 'practical godliness.' An ocean away from the nearest bishop, the Anglican churches of Virginia were scarcely less congregational in governance than the churches of New England.

By the beginning of the eighteenth century Virginians shared with New England more than just a growing secularism. Concepts of human nature, the process and character of historical change, the proper organization of society, and a broad view of American superiority were also held in common. The sense of American mission which Cotton Mather expressed in his writings was closely related to that of Robert Beverly, whose *History of Virginia* was one of the first expressions of the nascent American self-consciousness in the southern colonies.

Virginians' identity, like that of the Puritans', had been forged and tempered in the crucible of the American wilderness. These new Americans had also been sorely disappointed, and more than a little disillusioned, by what they had encountered in the New World. Nevertheless, by 1624, after incredible hardships and disappointments, an agricultural settlement with prospects for the future had taken root. Unable to locate any gold, the original Virginia Company had decided that the only commodity of value in the New World was

land. Hence, it began to recruit settlers instead of adventurers by holding out the promise of land ownership, a relatively rare occurrence among lower-class Englishmen. The company believed that land taxes and the sale of provisions to new settlers would provide profits. As it turned out, little or no profit was forthcoming and in 1624 the company went bankrupt. But Virginia had been transformed from a trading post into a colony which would continue to grow. Some of those who had survived the ordeal, or who remained in Virginia as settlers, grew wealthy and influential. In the process they helped formulate and give substance to the idea that they had in some special way been blessed for success. They had given themselves to the land, and the land in return had provided them with spiritual, social, economic, and political independence. Tobacco took the place of gold and the earth was the mine which endlessly produced rich bounty.

Virginia and Massachusetts were only the first two colonies in the New World to which men, women, and children of the Old World migrated. The ethnic and religious composition of the other colonies was more diverse than in the oldest colonies. The ties to the land and the sense of mission of the settlers in the younger colonies, however, if less obvious than those of the colonists in Massachusetts and Virginia, were no less strong.

❧❧❧

The colonists' sense of mission remained strong throughout the seventeenth and eighteenth centuries. As religious practices and institutions changed considerably, so, too, did the nature and role of colonial government. For example, from about 1680 to 1720 the structural forms of local government crystallized. Then between 1720 and 1760 provincial legislatures achieved maturity in the management of public affairs. Finally, between 1765 and 1790 a series of national congresses or conventions were held which helped to expand the dimensions of domestic politics once again.

To the colonists, the English constitution denoted the original principles that underlay their governments and their lives. Such principles included the idea that free men were bound only by laws to which they had consented, that private interests ought not to be set in opposition to the public good, and that the welfare of the whole community was the primary goal. Often Americans used the word *constitution* to refer to the limits society placed on its rulers. For them, power and authority were different concepts. The former represented absolute force; the latter was power sanctioned by right. The authority of government did not include the power to invade fundamental human rights.

This faith in the English constitution was reflected in the colonists' own local governments. In New England, for example, Puritan theorists had captured the essence of the constitution in their emphasis on compacts and covenants. Consequently, they contended that the power of the ruler should be exercised in accordance with established fundamental law, and that the government owed its existence to the consent of the governed.

In the more secular Virginia, the relationship between local theories of government and the English constitution was even more direct. Virginians believed with John Locke that man had been born an innocent in a state of nature, and in accordance with the laws of nature (or of God), man had been endowed with unalienable rights to life, liberty, and property. But in the natural state the strong tended to prey upon the weak, and so men formed themselves into societies and created governments. Governments, therefore, existed by virtue of voluntary agreements, or contracts, between the governed and the governors; their function was to protect the individual's natural rights to life, liberty, and property. If a ruler broke the contract by depriving the people of these rights, they would have no recourse but to overthrow that ruler, and establish a new contract with a new sovereign more likely to abide by his agreements.

Those who wielded power in both Virginia and New England were 'servants of society' or 'ministers of God' and as such had to be specially qualified: they had to be acquainted with the affairs of men, have wisdom, knowledge, and prudence, and be men of virtue and true principles. Such men did not seek office because they did not need office. Independent in wealth and opinion, ideally they could not be bought or otherwise corrupted.

It was a rule of political life in all the colonies that government was the legitimate concern only of those who possessed what was commonly called 'a stake in society.' By this stake in society one usually meant the possession of land, for the protection of which government had been originally formed. Those who owned land (or in some cases personal property of an equivalent value) were entitled to a voice in government.

The most common element in the American colonial mind was love of land, for the colonists were, at bottom, an agrarian people. The land provided them with food and sustenance, formed the basis of human welfare, created wealth, and, above all else, was the foundation of liberty—economic, social, and political. Most of the colonists had come to America poor and landless men. But once arrived, even without capital, they had managed to obtain land relatively easily. They had cultivated it and had earned economic security and independence by it. A large proportion of the immigrants to America became successful farmers and freed themselves from poverty and landlords. Merchants, craftsmen, and seamen also often purchased land for the respectability and power it conveyed.

Landholders in the colonies readily accepted the idea that agriculture was the basis of society and the source of all progress. They considered their occupation—working the soil—as the one indispensable industry. Their almanacs reinforced these views by assuring farmers of their own importance and good fortune and of the valuable role they played. Their daily lives also reinforced the importance of agriculture and added to their fear of cities and of any principles not based on the fact that property equalled land, and land equalled happiness. Thus, it should not be surprising that the colonists fashioned a system of governmental representation to serve the needs of their particular landed and agrarian interests.

Most settlers in America, especially those in New England, were by inheritance suspicious of power in the hands of kings, aristocrats, priests, and churches. But they were equally suspicious of power in the hands of the people. Women could not vote, nor could blacks, nor anyone under twenty-one. Property and residence requirements further restricted the franchise. Rule by simple majority would have been regarded as divisive and illegitimate.

The freehold qualifications for voting and holding

office which had prevailed in the counties of England for three hundred years prevailed in the colonies as well. The crucial difference, however, was that ownership of land—and thus qualification for the franchise—was far more widespread in America than in England. In America, freehold tenure became almost universal among the white population.

As time passed, the landed in all the colonies continued to exercise the franchise, but increasingly, because of higher property qualifications, only the wealthiest of the gentry could run for office. This system rested on a natural community of interest. Representatives and constituents in local colonial politics tended to agree on most issues. Thus, obedience to and respect for the legislatures usually followed. The colonists considered obedience not only to be their duty but to be in their best interests as well. In general, Americans consented to laws and taxes framed by their own representatives in their own legislatures, but balked at accepting arbitrary decrees.

Parliament, the major force in English politics, initially affected colonial life only peripherally. It dealt with matters obviously beyond the competence of any lesser authority and made a final review of actions initiated and sustained by colonial authorities. But all other powers were enjoyed, in fact if not in constitutional theory, by local governments. Parliament and the crown failed to recognize this unique situation and continued to function as if the colonists understood and accepted the realities of eighteenth-century political life in England. They expected the Acts of Trade and Navigation, which were designed to regulate commerce and the internal economics of the empire, to be enforced and obeyed. In doing so they created a code of laws and institutions applicable to American Englishmen to which the residents of England were not themselves subject. Although theory held that the empire was one society on two sides of the water, the colonists increasingly perceived that the scales were grossly imbalanced in favor of the mother country. The imperial structure of crown, Privy Council, Board of Trade, royal officials, and Vice-Admiralty Courts formed the basis for much discontent. Officials were generally slipshod, inefficient, and negligent in executing their duties. The royal governors, for example, often failed to perform their proper duties in the imperial system because they normally received their salaries from the local legislatures and thus tended out of self-interest to identify themselves with the colonials.

Over the course of many decades, an independent American attitude developed which played a major role in rearranging official imperial economic policies to suit the colonists' needs and conditions in the eighteenth century. Indeed, the colonists demonstrated a remarkable determination to have a voice in the management of their own economic destinies, for they perceived their role within Britain's mercantile system somewhat differently than did the British.

In general, Britain's mercantile system sought to increase the flow of public revenues and to foster the industrial growth of the mother country. As set down in the Acts of Trade and Navigation, the system was designed to provide control of colonial markets and a dependable supply of raw materials and other commodities. The colonists, however, almost immediately perceived that the economic principles under which the British operated involved some crucial inequities. They saw that while the colonies apparently existed for the welfare of the mother country, they were expected to be self-sufficient. Thus, the colonists knew that to carry their weight properly in the system they would have to disobey certain rules and regulations of the system.

Since laws to sustain mercantilism invariably sought to prohibit something that the colonists had found to be profitable, the task of enforcement proved extremely difficult. Two conditions plagued the system from the beginning. The first was geographical: America was simply too vast for an efficient supervision of trade. The other difficulty was institutional: England had, as yet, no tradition of civil service, royal or parliamentary, in the colonies or at home. Posts were filled more often through influence, bribery, or other corrupt means than through regard for honest and efficient administration. Consequently, the imperial commercial system worked when it was to the mutual advantage of the colonies and the mother country to abide by it. Otherwise, it was generally ignored.

Another problem inherent in the colonial system was the scarcity of a circulating medium, or money. In the beginning commodities often served as a local medium.

Some colonial assemblies made tobacco, sugar, or wheat legal tender at fixed values for the discharge of public and private debts. But commodity money failed to satisfy the monetary demands of a rapidly growing population trying to function as an integral part of a mercantilist system. As a result, by the beginning of the eighteenth century the problem of providing a domestic circulating medium had become an acute one in several of the provinces.

One cause of the perennial money shortage resulted from the high cost of local government, especially the requirements of military support. For a century or more, the colonists spent much of their time, energy, and wealth in making war on their neighbors, the Indians or the French or both. Demands for funds during these wars greatly inflated taxes in the colonies, and government was soon forced to find other expedients to finance military operations. In England, these wars fostered a 'Financial Revolution,' which produced central banking and created and monetized the public debt. The long (1721–1742) and astonishingly successful ministerial tenure of Sir Robert Walpole witnessed regularization of this financial system.

The lack of specie, the underdeveloped state of the economy, the impact of British imperial policy, and the controlling influence of British merchant creditors prevented any such 'Financial Revolution' from occurring in the colonies as well. To support the heavy burden of military expenses and other public demands, the individual colonies developed instead a system of forced short-term lending by issuing notes, or bills of credit, in anticipation of future tax returns. As for long-term public credit, the colonists created land banks which issued paper money in the form of loans against land ownership. This system provided liquid money for those whose assets were locked up in real estate. Deeply suspicious of banks and other financial institutions, the colonists believed private land banks to be a workable solution to their problems.

Land banks and bills of credit did not eliminate all money problems, however. For instance, the volume of paper money in circulation bore at best only a remote relationship to the actual needs of trade. Part of the reason for this was that no one knew precisely how values of paper money were to be measured, and how they were to be controlled. But the most important cause of improper money circulation was that each colony determined financial policy in response to the costs of war and government, and not according to principles of economic orthodoxy.

The colonists, nevertheless, believed their own currency systems worked well enough. Besides, they felt that only by remaining free of English financial machinations did they have any chance of surviving economically. Thus by creating land banks and a system of 'currency finance' which used bills of exchange, bills of credit, and other forms of public and private money, they managed to cover the rising costs of administration and war, and to provide a public source of agricultural and business credit independent of England and its new financial order. Most colonists recognized that there had to be enough currency in the system to cover the exchange of goods, ease the payment of domestic debts, and provide for a flexible economy. They believed that only local government had sufficient knowledge to understand local economic problems and deal with them correctly.

The colonists' desire to pursue economic policies independently was reinforced when they began to perceive that certain aspects of the Financial Revolution had begun to affect their economic well-being. They saw that after mid-century they had become dependent on British 'loans' for closing the gap in the balance of payments. They therefore became increasingly sensitive to fluctuations in British credit and capital markets. As a means to divorce themselves from the market fluctuations, the colonists relied more and more heavily on local currency systems to provide liquidity and protect their interests.

These actions forced the Board of Trade and Parliament to insist on more control, which further heightened the colonists' suspicion of a British conspiracy against their economic interests, represented most vividly in the passage of the Currency acts of 1751 and 1764. Such suspicions were voiced by gentry, farmers, traders, and professionals alike. The American farmer, for example, fiercely resented any interference in the cash flow which provided him with the lifeblood of his agricultural enterprise. Frontiersmen also produced goods or services of market value. Hence access to a steady cash flow was essential for colonial gentry, shopkeepers, traders, farmers, and frontiersmen, whose primary interests were commercial.

The new financial system in England, the colonists believed, had been behind the sudden shifts of monetary policies in the 1740s and the Currency acts later on. They were convinced that those 'money men' who had gained control of England's economic and political system during Walpole's ministry were now intent on doing the same in America. Such beliefs found powerful reinforcement in the works of Henry St. John, Viscount Bolingbroke, the great reactionary Tory theorist and writer, who saw nothing but decay and evil in eighteenth-century English life. He considered the Financial Revolution the poisonous fountainhead of it all, and he pleaded for a return to original principles and to the values of Britain's ancient constitution. In earlier times, Bolingbroke asserted, honor, manly virtue, and public spirit governed people's conduct, and effeminacy and luxury had been considered cardinal vices.

Bolingbroke's writings complemented those of the popular ancients, Livy, Cicero, Sallust, and Tacitus, who also spoke of an earlier, more virtuous age. The Americans agreed with the wistful praise of earlier and simpler societies, and regarded the emerging financial system in Britain as corrupt and degenerate. The widely read seventeenth-century English writers Sydney, Locke, Milton, and Harrington also wrote of earlier, more virtuous societies and reinforced the colonists' view of a degenerating modern England. Moreover, these so-called Commonwealthmen offered historical, legal, and ideological support for the 'rights of Englishmen' and the resurrection of original principles. Accordingly, they strengthened the firmly held belief that America and its inhabitants had a special destiny and represented the world's last hope for liberty, for it was believed that that system and those principles still thrived in the colonies. Eighteenth-century oppositionists, such as Burgh, Trenchard, Gordon, and especially Bolingbroke, reiterated the themes of man's lust for power, the assaults on the ancient constitution, and the crown's prerogative. They also added the new financial order to this list of 'evils.' Thus they spoke directly to the contemporary fears of the colonists and became extremely popular.

This cluster of ideas that the colonists would apply over and over again to their own situation respecting England became in America a 'Gospel of Opposition.' Not until Thomas Jefferson incorporated it into his Republican Revolution of 1800, would it lose its essentially oppositionist nature. The Gospel of Opposition had been promoted in England by no more than a handful of highly vocal but relatively powerless men. In the colonies, however, the litany was widely accepted, and became a cornerstone for the foundation of an American ideology because it was so deeply rooted in the celebration of simple, agrarian virtues. The Americans found encouragement in the Gospel of Opposition for it seemed to them to justify their conduct, rationalize their freedom of action, and give purpose to their lives.

Although the colonists believed that America had avoided the 'corruptions' of the Financial Revolution, and thus mirrored some idyllic English past, they considered a constant state of vigilance to be essential, for corruption was like a cancer and could overwhelm virtue. To remind themselves to be vigilant, they read and wrote history—a surprising amount of it about their own land. Adventurers and settlers wrote descriptions of the country, like those of Capt. John Smith of Virginia; they wrote of explorations and discoveries, of Indian wars and captivities; and they often wrote memoirs of their collective religious or political experiences. These local histories were often literary manifestations of a nascent American self-consciousness, a realization that American society was different from and superior to other societies. It was not yet nationalism that they expressed, for none of these historians thought of the colonies as a separate nation. But the colonists did think of their settlements as peculiarly blessed, and therefore the history of their appearance, growth, and singular virtue became a matter for deep historical study.

The metaphor most often encountered in the colonial literature, in histories as well as journals, sermons, verse, or travellers' accounts, was the cornucopia. This theme denoted an intense preoccupation with the abundance of the land. Not only did the writers constantly reiterate the idea of plenty, but they communicated a profound sense of reborn men winning victories over nature.

This self-awareness received crucial reinforcement

9

from the commonly accepted belief that constitutionalism and liberty thrived only in America. As early as 1735, the Englishman James Thomson had celebrated this idea in his book-length poem *Liberty*. The idea that liberty had been drifting steadily westward to America could also be seen in the opening section of Massachusetts Gov. Thomas Pownall's *Administration of the Colonies* (1764). Pownall had long assumed that the colonies would 'become in some future and perhaps not very distant age an asylum for . . . liberty . . . which, as it hath been driven by corruption, and the tyranny of government hath been constantly retiring westward.' Thomas Paine expressed it most passionately when he wrote, 'Let every lover of mankind, every hater of tyranny stand forth! Every spot of the old world is overrun with oppression. Freedom hath been hunted round the globe. Asia and Africa have long expelled her. Europe regards her like a stranger, and England hath given her warning to depart. O' receive the fugitive, and prepare in time an asylum for mankind.'

During the 1750s and 1760s expansionists like Benjamin Franklin, Archibald Kennedy, Lewis Evans, and others began to maintain that Anglo-Americans had a manifest destiny to dominate the continent. Franklin especially rhapsodized about the future glory and growth of America in his *Observations concerning the Increase of Mankind and the Peopling of Countries*. He was joined by John Adams who saw America in the early 1760s as having been chosen by God to bring happiness to mankind. 'I always consider the settlement of America with reverence and wonder,' he wrote, 'as the opening of a grand scene and design in Providence for the illumination of the ignorant and the emancipation of the slavish part of mankind all over the earth.' Beliefs such as these gave a powerful impetus to the colonists' resistance to British policies.

❧

In the years between the French and Indian War and the American Revolution, the colonists not only thought of themselves as being different from their English cousins but also as being entitled to the respect due a people that had arrived at political, economic, and cultural maturity. They gained confidence and strength during

these years of controversy. The struggle over the regulation of commerce, over taxation, and over constitutional authority convinced the colonists that, though they shared the same king, Englishmen and Americans were no longer part of the same society.

Increasingly, colonial oppositionists asserted that Great Britain was jealous of America's rising population, prosperity, and greatness; that she would never exercise government for the colonists' benefit; and that the only permanent security for American happiness was to deny Britain the power to transfer her financial system and corrupt arbitrary government to America. To do this, they argued, the knot which connected the two countries must be severed, for only then could American economic independence be ensured and ancient constitutional liberties be preserved.

British policy during these years seemed to lend credence to these arguments. King George III, who had ascended the throne in 1760, desired to play a larger role in government affairs than had his recent predecessors. Accordingly he manipulated royal patronage and controlled parliamentary elections so as to reestablish by political maneuvering the royal influence that earlier monarchs had exercised by right. Unfortunately for him, he picked ministers who were singularly inept and inflexible in dealing with the colonists.

Meanwhile, Parliament, needing revenue to pay off the large debt incurred during the French and Indian War, had turned to the colonists, who, compared with English landowners, were lightly taxed. It seemed only just that the Americans share some of the heavy burden laid on English taxpayers for the defense of American territory. Consequently, Parliament passed a series of regulations which intervened in the Atlantic economy at a time of great internal structural change. These measures affected the financial and social order of the colonies, and the colonial economic and political leaders responded accordingly.

The new imperial policy was inaugurated by George Grenville's ministry and continued by Charles Townshend and Lord North. From 1763 to 1765, Grenville established a permanent military force in the colonies, transferred the control over Indian relations from the colonial governments to imperial officials, restricted the advance of settlement on the western frontier, required the colonists to purchase revenue stamps, and forbade the colonial assemblies from issuing paper money. In 1767, Townshend pushed through Parliament a series of acts designed to raise revenue on a class of previously untaxed articles. Colonial nonimportation agreements eventually forced Parliament to repeal some of these measures. But such actions and responses as the Boston Massacre of 1770, Lord North's Tea Act of 1773, the Boston Tea Party, the 'Coercive Acts,' the Quartering Act, and the Quebec Act afforded committees of correspondence and the Sons of Liberty ample fuel for the flames of revolt.

To the colonists, all of these measures, as well as the reactions to the colonial protests that they inspired, clearly revealed a pattern of economic and political tyranny. Not all colonies reacted the same way to the earlier measures. Pennsylvanians, for example, were most disturbed by the Proclamation of 1763, New Yorkers by the Quartering Act, New Englanders by the Sugar Act, and Virginians by the Currency Act. But when Parliament passed the Stamp Act of 1765 and the Townshend Acts of 1767, the colonists developed a united resistance. The explosion of protest which accompanied these parliamentary acts indicated not only colonial aversion to taxation by Parliament, but also demonstrated a firm attachment to the British constitution and to home rule.

Economic changes added to the colonists' woes. The widening gap between imports and exports and an increasing reliance on British credit had placed enormous strains on the colonial monetary system. Spiralling exchange rates after 1763 and increased demand for liquidity also severely affected the economy. But the most psychologically significant economic problem, tumbling realty prices, threatened to undermine the very basis of American life, for American political, economic, and social traditions were all founded upon the availability and widespread ownership of land.

Until Parliament began to pass legislation which directly affected American economic, political, and social stability, the colonists' concern about the new financial order in England was confined to lamentations and other expressions of regret. When it became obvious from the pattern of British policies after 1763 that the British were trying to extend their 'wretched system' to America, the colonists resisted without hesitation. By implication, all the people of England were responsible for the economic tyranny, not just Parliament or the ministry. Accordingly, the colonists were certain that America had become the last dwelling place on earth of liberty, and that their liberty had to be preserved at all costs.

The New England clergy were among those who took the lead in warning the people of Britain's evil designs. In dozens of election sermons and other orations, they bitterly attacked the subversion of American 'Rights, Liberties and Privileges.' These sermons decried British tyranny, for the ministers were convinced that their ancestors had fled England to avoid similar oppression. They feared that the mother country had become even more corrupt than she had been under Charles II, and their sermons reflected this growing fear.

The New England clergy particularly feared the possible extension of the Anglican episcopacy to the American colonies (there were as yet no bishops resident in the colonies). In particular, they pointed toward the Society for the Propagation of the Gospel in Foreign Parts—an arm of the church created in 1701 to convert the Indians to Christianity—as an instrument of British tyranny. Preachers and politicians alike argued that this society had long had a formal design to root out Calvinist communions and to establish the Anglican Church throughout the colonies. They considered the extension of the authoritarian Anglican episcopacy to America to be only a prelude to an attempt to extend the rest of England's corrupt and perverted financial and political system to the colonies. There was opposition to the Anglican plan even in Virginia, where the people had gotten along very well without resident bishops. American bishops, the Virginians thought, represented a needless burden and would diminish the colonists' own authority.

Resistance to British designs would serve even broader purposes, according to the clergy; not only would it provide the chance to escape the worst aspects of the new social and economic order of England, it would also purify and revitalize the colonies and renew the colonists' slipping virtue. The most effective sermons—like those of Jonathan Mayhew, Charles Chauncy, Samuel Cook, William Gordon, and Samuel Langdon—

imparted a sense of crisis by reiterating Old Testament condemnations of a degenerate people. The clergy predicted that if something were not done to stem the advancing tide of moral degeneration, future Americans might prove to be the same sort of vile and depraved creatures that had succumbed to tyranny in Britain. The clergy worried that an increasing urbanity and ease had brought a relaxation of religious vigor. They believed that urban growth and commercial expansion, both at home and in trade overseas, had introduced corrupting influences. They were especially quick to condemn evils which lurked in cities, for it was through cities that the corruption, vice, and greed of England's economic and social system would enter. By fighting these evils through methods such as nonimportation, perhaps Americans could regain that purity they had had in earlier years and preserve the virtue and liberty which remained.

In the 1760s and '70s, Americans turned to the political sphere for a solution to their problems. In so doing, they integrated religious, economic, social, and political thinking into a revolutionary ideology which in the end persuaded them to seek complete independence from Britain. American revolutionary ideology was a body of thought that had been taken largely from the oppositionist tradition of seventeenth- and eighteenth-century England, as has been pointed out. The implication of much of this ideology was reactionary, for it opposed the new, depersonalized world of money, machines, cities, and excessive government. The ideologues of the American Revolution, though often characterized by the English as dangerous innovators, tended, like the early oppositionists in England, to resist the emergence of the modern world. They believed the 'wicked ministry' of George III to be attempting to transform, control, and corrupt America, just as the English oppositionists had believed Walpole and the new monied classes to be transforming and corrupting England.

American oppositionists—men like George Mason, John Dickinson, Benjamin Franklin, Richard Bland, James Wilson, James Otis, and Thomas Jefferson— agreed that although the English had apparently squandered their birthright, liberty still thrived in the colonies. Because the colonists were repeatedly told by English and American oppositionists that they represented the last outpost of English liberty and virtue, they labored under a double obligation. They had to preserve their own virtue, and in so doing fulfill their special destiny as a beacon for the rest of mankind. American allegiance to virtue was no lonely thing, no solitary worship of God, no hermit-like renunciation, no agonized striving for purity and salvation. It was much more. It was obedience to those long-established religious, social, economic, and political relationships upon which the colonists had so carefully constructed a way of life, and over which they believed a kindly Deity smiled benevolently and protectively; for the happiness of all His Creation existed in, and would be dependent upon, America.

The Americans believed themselves heirs to the liberties and traditions of Englishmen. They wanted to preserve those, and in so doing, serve as a model for the rest of the world. The colonists, therefore, mixed their self-interest with high moral purpose, natural and religious law, and their own mythology of an American Eden, and created a rebellion. They were not about to allow their Canaan to be debauched without a fight to the death. The final rush of events leading up to the fateful day of Lexington and Concord, April 19, 1775, persuaded them to take up arms to defend their liberties. The ultimate logic of their rebellion (expressed so vividly in Thomas Paine's *Common Sense*) was independence, which their representatives voted on July 2, 1776, and approved formally on July 4.

The most revolutionary aspect of the American Revolution was political. The Americans severed their bonds with their king, overthrew their governments, ousted the opponents of the Revolution and confiscated their property, and created the mechanisms by which the people were deemed to act as the sovereign power. The abstract doctrine of the 'sovereignty of the people' had been 'reduced to practice,' as John Adams put it, 'by assemblages of fairly level headed Gentlemen exercising constituent power in the name of the People.' In short, the Americans had given birth to thirteen republics.

Nonetheless, the political ideas ratified the concept of representative bodies as mirrors of their constituents, of natural law limiting man-made law, of constitutions as ideal designs for government, and of sovereignty as divisible. They were at once both expressive of conditions that had long existed in the colonies, and a basic reiteration of the original principles of government and society as found in the English constitution. Indeed, American leaders very carefully pointed out that a 'republic' formed the very foundation of the ancient British constitution, and was therefore the best of governments.

John Adams argued that the most valuable part of the British constitution had been its predominant republicanism. Adams, like many other Americans, believed that a man could be both a monarchist and a republican if the monarch maintained his role as first magistrate in an empire of laws. Unfortunately, the empire of laws in England had been perverted and the republican constitutional balance had been destroyed. By revolting, Adams believed, the Americans had thwarted Britain's attempt to destroy traditional American republicanism.

The American Revolution was a most unorthodox upheaval. American society after the Revolution, in spite of obvious political innovations, remained consciously traditional and conservative. The colonists had not been discontent with conditions as they appeared before the 1760s. Instead they wanted to preserve them. The English, as the Americans saw it, had been the ones who had tried to disrupt the status quo, and it had been those attempts which had precipitated the rebellion. For the Americans, revolution was a way not of destroying, but of preserving and strengthening an existing social order. With the achievement of their Revolution, the Americans had given a new secular meaning to the mission which John Winthrop had stated in religious terms a century and a half before, that of being 'as a City upon a Hill.'

❧

During the Revolution, the colonies adopted as their instrument of government the Articles of Confederation, which bound the thirteen states together in little more than a league of friendship, presided over by a congress with severely limited powers. The greatest achievement of the Confederation Congress was the Northwest Ordinance of 1787, which created a great national domain west of the Appalachian Mountains and formulated the system for land sales and territorial government by which the nation expanded. The Confederation's weaknesses heavily outweighed its strengths, however. To some observers, the Confederation's failures made America laughable in the eyes of Europeans, thus jeopardizing the success of the American mission to be the model for the world. In 1787, a convention met in Philadelphia to draw up a new plan of government for the United States. The delegates tended to be merchants desiring uniform commercial policies, artisans and manufacturers wanting uniform tariffs, and frontiersmen seeking more vigorous defense against the Indians, Spanish, or British. They were joined by creditors who sought protection against debtor legislation, paper money, and the assaults of the unpropertied on the sanctity of property.

Despite many differences which surfaced during the convention, a spirit of compromise prevailed. After four months of deliberation, the delegates created a document which reconciled the views of the nationalists and those who favored a looser, confederated system. The Constitution's basic feature was the creation of a 'federal' system in which powers and responsibilities were distributed between the state and national governments.

The final document was a remarkable piece of work. Though innovative by its very nature, it had been designed principally to control the social forces the Revolution had released. The framers of the Constitution had few illusions about the 'rationality of the generality of mankind.' After Shays's Rebellion and other examples of social unrest, the delegates feared more than ever the 'giddiness of the multitude.' They worked diligently to fashion a system of government which would prevent social anarchy and save the republican experiment in America.

To the Federalists, as the supporters of the new Constitution became known, it appeared evident that, if the public good was to be achieved, and if the 'worthy' were to be protected from the 'licentious,' the American people had to be on guard against certain potential excesses of the Revolution, such as a too-great reliance on the broadly representative state legislatures, and place their confidence once again in the natural leaders of the society. The Federalists had not lost faith in the people's ability to discern their true leaders. In fact, most had confidence that the people, if properly directed, would continually elect the 'proper sort.' They viewed the Constitution as a device to exercise such direction. The Federalists argued that under the new federal scheme, power would gravitate to men who would pursue vigorously what they perceived to be the best interests of the whole country. They would be free of the clamors of 'men of factious tempers, of local prejudices, or of sinister designs.'

Alexander Hamilton of New York provided the ideological underpinnings for the constitutional system in article number 35 of *The Federalist*. Hamilton's view of society was holistic: all the diverse elements of the society were of a piece; that is, all ranks and degrees of men were connected in such a way that those on the top were necessarily involved in the welfare of those below them. This philosophy was not new, for it lay at the heart of the Anglo-American agrarian ethic and had been a crucial element in the Gospel of Opposition.

The Federalists, of course, never claimed to be repudiating the Revolution or republicanism, but saw themselves as saving both from their own excesses. As the Federalists saw it, republican government was a terribly fragile institution. It was so difficult to maintain that only expert and accountable elites could save it from degenerating either into despotism at one extreme or anarchy at the other. In short, the Federalists believed the Constitution would reaffirm and strengthen the original principles upon which America had been founded and maintained. It would provide the necessary institutional framework for achieving the original goals of the Revolution: a stable and orderly government in which men (despite their imperfections) were free to enjoy the blessings of liberty and independence, and the security of property that was so essential a part of those blessings.

The Constitution went before the people in the states for ratification in September 1787. A strong opposition developed that came quite close to thwarting the objectives of the Federalists. The Federalists faced a serious challenge. Their chief task was to refute the charge of their opponents, the 'Antifederalists,' that their handiwork was an instrument by which aristocrats or mon-

archists plotted to steal the fruits of the Revolution from the people. A remarkable intellectual battle broke out in the newspapers and in pamphlets. Between October 27, 1787, and April 4, 1788, Alexander Hamilton, James Madison, and John Jay, using the joint pen name 'Publius,' published a series of brilliant letters in the *Independent Journal* of New York in defense of the Constitution. Later brought out in two volumes as *The Federalist*, their work provided a lucid explanation of the new document and drew adherents to the Constitution.

Five states—Delaware, Pennsylvania, New Jersey, Georgia, and Connecticut—ratified the Constitution speedily, between December 7, 1787, and January 9, 1788. In Massachusetts, the sixth state to ratify, respected figures like John Hancock and Samuel Adams had objected to the absence from the Constitution of a bill of rights. The Massachusetts convention thus made ratification conditional on a promise to add a bill of rights.

That compromise spurred into action some of the states which still hesitated. Between April 28 and June 21, 1788, Maryland, South Carolina, and New Hampshire agreed to accept the new government. That brought the number of states ratifying to nine, the number required to make the Constitution effective. The fate of the new government, however, was still in doubt as long as Virginia and New York failed to act; each was large enough to assert its independence if it desired to do so. The failure of either to approve would have wrecked the scheme. Both states finally ratified June 26, 1788, although by narrow margins. North Carolina also agreed to the new government, but not before it had been in operation for several months. Rhode Island stood alone until Congress threatened to treat the recalcitrant state as alien territory. Rhode Island finally ratified, in May 1790. The United States of America, under its unique Constitution, was now ready to consolidate its great experiment in republicanism.

❧

To no one's surprise, George Washington became the first president of the United States under the Constitution. The electors also chose the sturdy patriot John

Adams to be vice-president. When the first Congress met in New York's City Hall in April 1789, the Federalists dominated both houses. Soon, a tariff act was passed to provide income for the national government. The creation of the departments of state, treasury, and war provided organization for the executive branch. The Judiciary Act of 1789 organized the Supreme Court, created an appellate court system, and provided for an attorney general. The first Congress also adopted the first ten amendments to the Constitution, known collectively as the Bill of Rights.

Washington appointed Alexander Hamilton secretary of the treasury and Thomas Jefferson secretary of state. These two men, along with the secretary of war, Henry Knox, and the attorney general, Edmund Randolph, constituted the cabinet, a major governmental institution nowhere mentioned in the Constitution. Of these men, Hamilton clearly dominated. His administrative genius and policies welded the nation together with bonds of economic interest; they provided for the management of public finances in a way that benefited all the elements of society. Hamilton did not consider his policies to be those of a narrow interest group, faction, or party. Rather, he believed them to be truly national policies, for they made the diverse elements of American society interdependent, as well as dependent upon the national government.

Hamilton tried to fashion a system that was not unlike that which began to emerge in England after the Glorious Revolution of 1688 and was brought to maturity by Sir Robert Walpole during the 1720s and 1730s. That system worked in part by tying the interests of the wealthy to those of the national government or, more accurately, by inducing people of all ranks to act in the general interest by making it profitable for them to do so.

The Hamiltonians initiated their policies by funding the national debt, assuming responsibility for the state debts, and establishing a national bank. As a result, a viable circulating medium was created, capitalists found sources for profitable investments, and, most importantly, the funded continental and state securities were converted into fluid and expendable capital. Accordingly, all elements of society became further bound to the new federal government, for no one could pursue

power and wealth successfully except through the framework of its institutions.

The most serious opposition to Hamilton's program came from Virginia and his fellow cabinet officer Thomas Jefferson. The Virginians had a deeply ingrained hostility to the urban, commercial, monetized way of life. Because of their great attachment to agrarianism they regarded anything that smacked of high finance as inherently corrupt and antirepublican. Finally, they deeply distrusted any form of government over which they felt they had no control, but which might exert control over their lives.

By 1791, agrarian-minded men, led by the Virginians Jefferson and Madison, formed a recognizable opposition to Hamilton's policies. This new faction drew some support from rising businessmen in the cities, and some from artisans in the towns, but it gained most of its strength from southern plantation owners and farmers isolated from the main channels of trade and communication. They regarded Hamilton's scheme as utterly wicked, just as the English oppositionists had regarded Walpole's system. Indeed, the Jeffersonians borrowed heavily from the Gospel of Opposition for their ideology.

Basic differences between Hamiltonians and Jeffersonians later surfaced in the arena of foreign affairs. Most Americans welcomed the French Revolution of 1789 with enthusiasm, for it confirmed their faith that their own Revolution would light the torch of liberty for all mankind. The execution of Louis XVI and the advent of the Reign of Terror in France, however, drove many Hamiltonian Federalists into hysterical fears of mob rule, atheism, and Jacobinism (French-style radicalism) at home.

The French Revolution also precipitated a great European war which lasted with brief interruptions from 1793 until 1815. On one side stood France and on the other stood a series of European coalitions headed by Great Britain. The United States owed a debt of gratitude to France and was bound officially to it by a 'permanent' treaty of friendship and alliance, signed in 1778. Nevertheless, when France, early in 1793, executed the king and declared war on Great Britain, Holland, and Spain, President Washington issued a proclamation of neutrality. The president's proclamation could not, however, compel Americans to be neutral in spirit. Throughout the 1790s—particularly after the controversy in 1794–1795 over Jay's Treaty—foreign affairs deeply divided the American people.

President Washington, scarred by the attacks of Jeffersonian newspaper 'scribblers,' did not stand for election to a third term in 1796. The electoral college mirrored the deep split among the political factions in the country: the Federalist John Adams became president and the Republican Jefferson vice-president. During the Adams presidency, the nation almost went to war with France and almost destroyed itself in civil war. John Adams must be credited with great courage and selflessness for resisting the war hysteria at the cost of his own popularity and the political success of his party. But he must also be held at least partially responsible for the Alien and Sedition Acts of 1798, and the increased partisan opposition that those acts aroused among the Jeffersonian Republicans. Adams had, in fact, supplied his political enemies with potent ammunition in his second battle for the presidency with Jefferson in 1800. Though the Republicans had been weakened by their ties with France, the reaction against the Alien and Sedition Acts gave them new life. This time Jefferson narrowly defeated Adams seventy-three electoral votes to sixty-five.

Jefferson called this triumph 'the Revolution of 1800,' and declared that it 'was as real a revolution in the principles of our government as that of 1776 was in form.' This new revolution had become necessary, according to the Republicans, because the American Revolution, like the Glorious Revolution of 1688–1689 in England before it, had failed of ultimate fulfillment. As the Republicans saw it, Hamiltonians had perverted the goals of the American Revolution in the same way that Walpole had those of 1688–1689. Both revolutions had been fought to check executive power, yet both ended in one of the potentially worst forms of executive tyranny—ministerial government. Artificial wealth not based on honest labor or land ownership had been the corrupting force in both cases. The people had been encouraged by government ministers to pursue easy wealth and a frenzy of stock jobbing, gambling, and paper shuffling had resulted. Thus, after both revolutions, manly virtue had succumbed to effeminacy and vice, and public spirit had fallen victim to corruption and venality.

The Republicans believed that they would restore America to its original principles, the same principles which had infused the spirit of 1776. Constitutional balance among the branches of government would be restored. The gentry and yeomanry would be restored to their traditional places of prestige and power. Commerce would resume its subordinate role to agriculture. In this undertaking, the Republicans had reason for hope, as the English dissidents had not, for the task could be accomplished within the framework of the Constitution. Under the Constitution, this republic could once more attempt to play out its exemplary role as the model for the world to emulate.

Stunning as the triumph of the Jeffersonians was, however, it did not spell total defeat for the Federalists or their policies. Although no Federalist ever again occupied the presidency, Federalists retained strength in certain areas, particularly in New England. Nor did the Jeffersonians completely dismantle the Hamiltonian financial system.

What had happened by 1801 was that two different social, political, and economic philosophies had become firmly established. Some historians have identified these threads as Jeffersonianism and Hamiltonianism; others as liberalism and conservatism. In 1800 these forces had reached a state of equilibrium; the year produced a transition from Hamiltonianism to Jeffersonianism. Adherents of both traditions have contended for national leadership since 1800, even as the nation has experienced profound social change. Through all of these shifts in policy, however, the sense of American mission, variously expressed as Manifest Destiny, the Crusade to Make the World Safe for Democracy, and other causes, has remained strong.

From wellsprings both in the Old and New World more than three centuries ago emerged a nation that has deeply influenced the history of the world. In no small part that influence has resulted from the strong sense of mission that led to the founding and growth of the colonies, and has been characteristic of the American way of life ever since.

Catalogue of the Exhibition

2. John Winthrop, the first governor of the Massachusetts Bay Company

The Independent Mind—Road to Revolution

SETTLEMENTS

Of the English settlements on the North American mainland in the early seventeenth century, the most important were established by the Puritans in New England. The Puritans believed that by emigrating to the New World they had been reborn and that the fate of the world now rested with them. This sense of mission stimulated social thought, for it became possible to contemplate the creation of a new social, political, and religious order. Accordingly, their early writings constantly focused on the utopian nature of their undertaking. The Puritans believed that they had a mission to recreate a simpler, purer Christian past and that the rest of mankind would follow their example.

Settlers in the other colonies also became absorbed by the belief that, in their new land, they had a unique mission and destiny. The concept received reinforcement from the writings of adventurers and settlers like Sir Walter Raleigh, John Smith, and William Penn, and received further support from the seemingly limitless supply of land available to those who had the courage, industry, and character to take advantage of it.

---

1 NATHANIEL MORTON (1613–1685)

New-Englands Memoriall: or A Brief Relation of the . . . Planters of New-England in America

Cambridge, Mass., 1669. Evans 144. Bequest of John W. Farwell, 1943.

Morton was the secretary of Plymouth colony and he drafted most of the colony's laws. He became the best-informed man on Pilgrim history and prepared this history at the request of the commissioners of the four New England colonies. The book is opened to Morton's account of the Mayflower Compact, which put into effective form the ancient and abiding feature of Anglo-Saxon freedom—government by the consent of the governed.

2

Portrait of John Winthrop (1588–1649)

Oil painting. Bequest of William Winthrop, 1830.

Winthrop was the principal organizer and first governor of the Massachusetts Bay Company. On March 22, 1630, Winthrop set sail for America, accompanied by six or seven hundred men, women, and children. By the end of 1630, six settlements had been established in Boston and its environs with nearly two thousand inhabitants.

This portrait was painted from life in England by an unknown artist of the school of Van Dyke.

3 JOHN FOSTER (1648–1681)

Portrait of Richard Mather (1596–1669)

Relief cut, ca. 1670. Bequest of William Bentley, 1819.

Mather was a leader of Congregationalism in Massachusetts and his *Church Government and Church Covenant Discussed* (1643) was the first elaborate defense and exposition of the New England theory of the church and its administration to be put forth in print. He also played a major role in the acceptance of the Halfway Covenant in 1657.

This portrait of Mather by John Foster is the first portrait print made in America and is based on an oil portrait in the collections of the Society.

4

A Platform of Church Discipline

Cambridge, Mass., 1649. Evans 25.

5   RICHARD MATHER (1596–1669)

A Modell of Church-Government

Manuscript, Mather Family Papers.

This document defined the essentials of Puritan church organization. In meetings from 1646 to 1648 a synod of ministers and laymen gathered at Cambridge to decide the form that church government would take in the new colony. The platform stressed system, organization, and legitimacy, three issues of pressing importance to the Puritan mission. It also emphasized the nature of the covenant made between the Puritans and God to be responsible for and to one another in their government of saints. This document, like the Mayflower Compact, was an early expression of independent self-government and represented the extension of church authority into the political sphere. Mather's original draft of the 'Cambridge Platform' is exhibited here next to the printed version.

6

The Whole Booke of Psalmes Faithfully Translated into English Metre

[Cambridge, Mass.], 1640. Evans 4.

This, the so-called Bay Psalm Book, is the first book printed in English America and is one of eleven known copies. Richard Mather, John Eliot, and Thomas Welde translated the psalms in meter to adapt them for singing during worship. It is significant that the first American imprint was a religious work designed to bring the congregations into closer

communication with God through the communal singing of psalms.

7   PETER PELHAM (ca. 1697–1751)

Portrait of Cotton Mather (1663–1728)

Oil painting, 1727. Gift of Mrs. Frederick Lewis Gay, 1923.

The son of Increase Mather and grandson of both Richard Mather and John Cotton, Mather played an important role in deposing Edmund Andros as governor of the Dominion of New England after the Glorious Revolution of 1688–1689 in England. Mather was a major American thinker of his time and wrote many theological tracts which emphasized the special destiny of America under Christ.

8   COTTON MATHER (1663–1728)

Magnalia Christi Americana

London, 1702. Bequest of John W. Farwell, 1943.

This book describes the flight of true Christianity from Europe to America where God's chosen people, the Puritans, would not only purify Protestantism but redeem mankind. Beyond the emphasis on the Puritan sense of mission, Mather's compilation included a vast amount of information on events, important personages, and political, social, and religious institutions.

9   COTTON MATHER (1663–1728)

Theopolis Americana

Boston, 1710. Evans 1469. Gift of Thomas Wallcut, 1834.

Mather's vision of a Holy City of pure gold is described in this sermon. He believed that such a city existed in America and that the Puritans, after proving their worthiness to God, were destined to find it and serve as a model for the rest of the world. Mather's views were shared by most of the Puritans.

Mr, Richard Mather.

3. Richard Mather, Puritan theorizer and administrator

THE

BLOVDY TENENT,

of PERSECUTION, for cause of CONSCIENCE, discussed, in

A Conference betweene

TRVTH and PEACE.

VVHO,

In all tender Affection, present to the High
Court of *Parliament*, (as the *Result* of
their *Discourse*) these, (amongst other
Passages) of highest consideration.

Printed in the Year 1644.

11. Roger Williams's tract on democratic principles and religious liberty

10

At a General Court Held at Boston the 16th of March 1680/81

[Boston, 1681.] Bristol 55. MP 39216.

This broadside, ordered printed by the General Court of Massachusetts Bay, announces a day of fasting and prayer to ask God's forgiveness for the transgressions of the people, transgressions which had caused the sufferings and hardships described herein. Those who survived such miseries were considered better for it, but entreaties were nevertheless made to God to insure order, peace, and just rulers.

11 ROGER WILLIAMS (1604?-1683)

The Bloudy Tenent, of Persecution

London, 1644.

After arriving in Massachusetts in 1631 Williams immediately gained notoriety by frankly criticizing the Puritan system. Forced out of Salem, he moved to Rhode Island with his followers in 1636. There he provided for religious liberty, complete separation of church and state, and liberal land policies. *The Bloudy Tenent*, his most celebrated work, asserted that all individuals and religious bodies were entitled to religious liberty as a natural right.

12 SAMUEL HARRIS (1783-1810)

Portrait of Sir Walter Raleigh (1552?-1618)

Red chalk drawing, ca. 1805. Bequest of William Bentley, 1819.

Raleigh was a military and naval commander, who, on the return of a preliminary expedition to the New World in 1584, christened the continent from Florida to Newfoundland Virginia. Though he never visited Virginia himself he helped promote the idea that this area of the world was a virtual paradise on earth.

The drawing was commissioned by William Bentley, a Salem clergyman. He had a large collection of portraits—prints, paintings, and drawings—of persons of historical importance.

13 JOHN SMITH (1580-1631)

The Generall Historie of Virginia, New-England, and the Summer Isles

London, 1627.

John Smith was an adventurer and explorer who took an active part in the promotion and organization of the Virginia Company of London, and served in an active capacity as leader of the original settlement. He also drew up a series of maps of the New World including New England. The accounts of his adventures, including the famous story of Pocahontas, are found in this history, which was a powerful agent in propagandizing to Englishmen the advantages of the New World.

14 WILLIAM PENN (1644-1718)

No Cross, No Crown

Boston, 1747. Evans 6041.

The founder of Pennsylvania, Penn wrote this tract (first published in London in 1669) while imprisoned in the Tower of London for publishing an unorthodox work. Presaging the ideologues of the American Revolution, he wrote against luxury, frivolity, money-madness, and economic oppression. He also favored and wrote about religious toleration, security of person and property, and other rights of Englishmen. This Boston printing is the first American edition.

15 ROBERT MORDEN (d. 1703)

A New Map of the English Empire in America

London, engraved by I. Harris, ca. 1695.

This map of the British colonies shows the pattern of early settlements along the Atlantic coast and rivers. Inland settlements were scarce because of the Indian menace and difficulty of travel over the mountains. But settlers, drawn by the easy availability of land and the promise of America's future, continued to make the Atlantic crossing.

12. Sir Walter Raleigh, adventurer and early promoter of the Virginia colony

PRINCIPLES, ORDER, AND LAW

Living in a wilderness three thousand miles from England and facing enormous obstacles to their survival, the colonists recognized the need for their governments to maintain law and order to ensure the survival of their mission. They insisted on having their original charters, covenants, compacts, and laws, which formed the basis for their governments, clearly spelled out in print. These early experiences in independent self-government provided Americans with a tradition of home rule which they would eventually fight a war to preserve.

16

The Records of the Council for New England. May 1622–June 1623

Manuscript. Gift of Frederick Lewis Gay, 1912.

The Council for New England was incorporated by the King of England, November 3, 1620, for 'the planting, ruling, and governing of New England in America.' For almost twenty years it administered New England; during that time nearly all the public documents relating to the region, such as orders, commissions, patents and grants of land, emanated from it. This manuscript is the only extant, original, record book of the Council.

17 JOHN COTTON (1584–1652)

An Abstract of Laws and Government

London, 1655. Bequest of John W. Farwell, 1943.

An early settler and leader of Massachusetts, Cotton wrote this abstract as a guide for mankind in general and New Englanders in particular. Though rejected by the General Court, the plan typifies the settlers' passion for legitimizing their society and providing it with system, order, and law. This copy belonged to Increase Mather, a second-generation Puritan and the author's son-in-law.

18

Rights of the Kingdom: or, Customs of Our Ancestors. Touching the Duty, Power, Election, or Succession of Our Kings and Parliaments

London, 1682.

This book, which belonged to Isaiah Thomas, was typical of those works the colonists owned which emphasized the long tradition of English liberty, a tradition of which they felt very much a part. Indeed, they considered themselves the rightful inheritors and preservers of the ancient Saxon constitution, and as such chosen by God for a special destiny.

19

The Charters of the Province of Pensilvania and City of Philadelphia

Philadelphia, 1742. Evans 5033.

Reprinted here are William Penn's original agreement with Charles II and the 'Charter of Privileges' granted by Penn to the inhabitants of Pennsylvania in 1681. The colonists cherished their rights and traditions and frequently referred to their original charters and compacts to reinforce their constitutional position in regard to England.

20 JACOB MELYEN (1639?–1706)

Letterbook, 1691–1696

Manuscript. Gift of Stephen Salisbury, 1900.

This letterbook of Jacob Melyen contains copies of eighty-eight letters. There is much material relating to Jacob Leisler's rebellion against the Dominion of New England, a rebellion triggered by the Glorious Revolution in England, and one which reestablished local rule for the colony of New York. Most colonists were generally relieved when William and Mary replaced James II on the throne, for they believed the Glorious Revolution had been a victory for the original principles of England's ancient constitution and therefore a victory for the principles upon which their own local governments had been founded. This belief is echoed in the formal 'God Save King William and Queen Mary,' which closes the declaration against Maj. Richard Ingoldsby, and in the salutation to the next document, also a protest against Ingoldsby.

21

A Copy of the King Majesties Charter, For Incorporating the Company of the Massachusets Bay in New-England in America

Boston, 1689. Evans 474.

22

The Charter Granted by His Majesty King Charles II. To The Governor and Company of The English Colony of Rhode-Island and Providence-Plantations

Newport, 1744. Evans 5683.

23

Laws of the Government of New-Castle, Kent and Sussex, Upon Delaware

Philadelphia, 1752. Evans 6835.

These volumes contain the original charters for Massachusetts Bay (1629), Rhode Island (1663), and Delaware (1701), as well as the laws passed in the latter two colonies up to 1744 and 1751 respectively. These imprints demonstrate the fundamental importance Americans attached to seeing the exact nature of their liberties and government spelled out on paper. Published laws, rules, and regulations assured the colonists of their connection with the liberties and traditions of Englishmen.

24

New-Haven's Settling in New-England. And Some Lawes for Government

London, 1656.

25

Several Rules, Orders, and By-Laws . . . of Boston

Boston, 1702. Evans 1040. Gift of Thomas Wallcut, 1834.

26

The Charter and the Several Laws, Orders & Ordinances . . . of the City of New-York

New York, 1719. Evans 2161. Gift of H. Dunscombe Colt, 1973.

These ordinances of local governments are examples of the colonists' realization of the need for laws and ordinances to govern themselves. The tradition extended back to the Mayflower Compact [1] and was an important consideration in framing the Constitution in 1787.

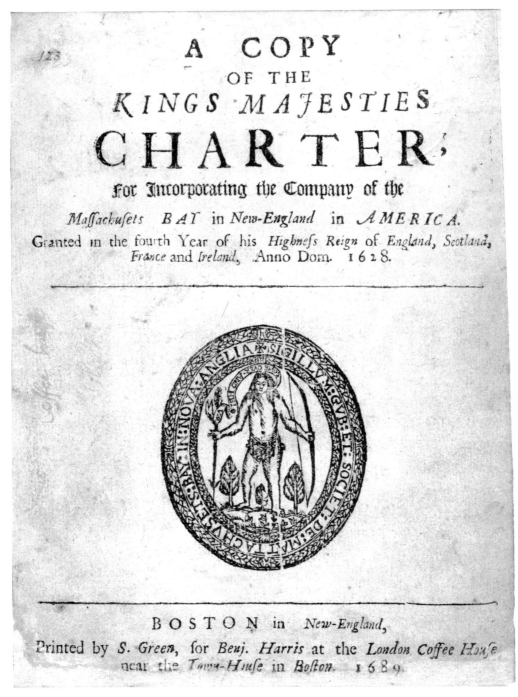

A COPY
OF THE
KINGS MAJESTIES
CHARTER,
for Incorporating the Company of the

Maſſachuſets BAY in New-England in AMERICA.
Granted in the fourth Year of his *Highneſs Reign* of *England, Scotland, France* and *Ireland,* Anno Dom. 1628.

BOSTON in *New-England,*
Printed by *S. Green,* for *Benj. Harris* at the *London Coffee Houſe* near the *Town-Houſe* in *Boſton.* 1689.

21. The original Massachusetts Bay Company charter

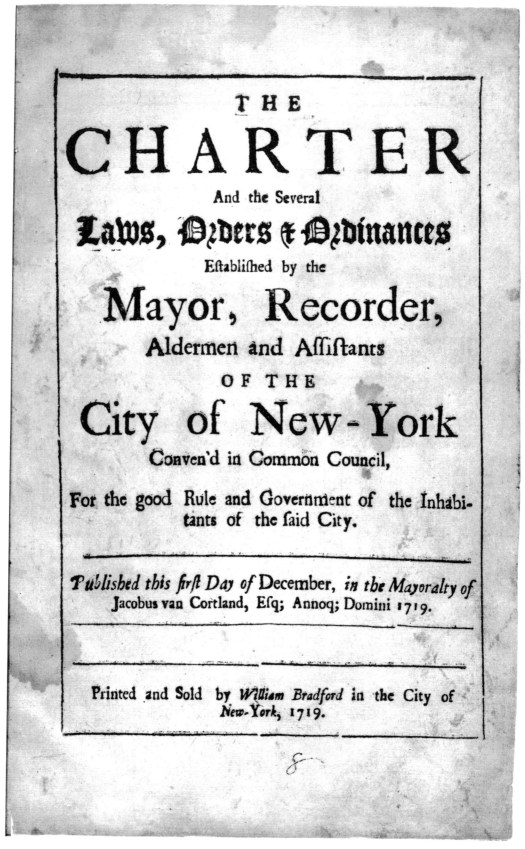

THE
CHARTER

And the Several

Laws, Orders & Ordinances

Established by the

Mayor, Recorder,

Aldermen and Assistants

OF THE

City of New-York

Conven'd in Common Council,

For the good Rule and Government of the Inhabitants of the said City.

Published this first Day of December, *in the Mayoralty of*
Jacobus van Cortland, Esq; Annoq; Domini 1719.

Printed and Sold by *William Bradford* in the City of
New-York, 1719.

26. Charter for the self-government of the city of New York

During the last quarter of the seventeenth century, the colonists spent much of their time, energy, and wealth making war on the Indians. Anglo-Americans generally viewed their neighbors as a threat to the completion of their mission and often as another element of nature to be subdued before their destiny could be secured. For a time, the official policy was to keep the natives as far away from white men as possible. From the 1630s to the 1660s the colonists were generally successful in implementing such a policy, for the Indians did not relish facing the devastating firepower of English muskets.

Some missionaries, led by John Eliot, did attempt to Christianize the Indians, and they even published an Indian-language version of the Bible. But most colonists believed the American natives to be the 'children of Satan.' Such conflicts as King Philip's War in 1675 and the war of the same year in Virginia, which precipitated the revolt against royal authorities known as Bacon's Rebellion, were viewed by most colonists as struggles between the forces of good and evil. They also believed that these conflicts had been designed by God to test the character and virtue of His favored children.

27

The Holy Bible: Containing the Old Testament and the New. Translated into the Indian Language

Cambridge, Mass., 1663. Evans 64 and 72.

Under the sponsorship of the Society for the Propagation of the Gospel, the missionary John Eliot preached to the Indians in their own language and translated the Bible into one of the Indian dialects. The New Testament was published in 1661 and the Old Testament in 1663. This was the first Bible to be printed in North America.

28 JOHN ELIOT (1604–1690)

A Late and Further Manifestation of the Progress of the Gospel Amongst the Indians in New-England

London, 1655. Gift of William Henry Bass, 1815.

Before the advent of King Philip's War in 1675 and the fixing of the view that all Indians were the 'devil's children,' a concerted effort to convert them was undertaken by a few Puritan missionaries, led by John Eliot. Among his activities was the establishment of several communities of 'praying Indians' in the interior of Massachusetts. This tract chronicles his progress to 1655. Unfortunately, whatever gains Eliot and his fellow missionaries made were obliterated by King Philip's War.

29 INCREASE MATHER (1639–1723)

A Brief History of the Warr with the Indians in New-England

Boston, 1676. Evans 220.

A Puritan clergyman, politician, and author, Increase Mather was the youngest son of Richard Mather. Some one hundred and thirty books and pamphlets written by him were published; two of those works were histories of the Indian wars. This pamphlet attempts to describe the colonists' ordeal with the Indians as a test instituted by God to try the mettle of the Puritans. That they were successful in their struggle proved their superior character and godliness, according to Mather.

30 WILLIAM HUBBARD (1621–1704)

A Narrative of the Troubles with the Indians in New-England

Boston, 1677. Evans 231. Bequest of John W. Farwell, 1943.

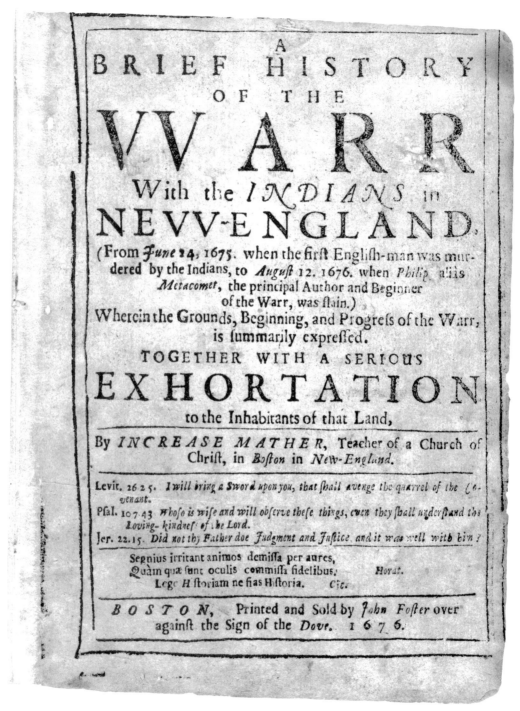

A
BRIEF HISTORY
OF THE
VVARR
With the *INDIANS* in
NEVV-ENGLAND.

(From *June* 24. 1675. when the first English-man was mur-
dered by the Indians, to *August* 12. 1676. when *Philip* alias
Metacomet, the principal Author and Beginner
of the Warr, was slain.)
Wherein the Grounds, Beginning, and Progress of the Warr,
is summarily expressed.

TOGETHER WITH A SERIOUS
EXHORTATION
to the Inhabitants of that Land,

By *INCREASE MATHER*, Teacher of a Church of
Christ, in *Boston* in *New-England.*

Levit. 26 25. *I will bring a Sword upon you, that shall avenge the quarrel of the Co-
venant.*
Psal. 107.43 *Whoso is wise and will observe these things, even they shall understand the
Loving-kindness of the Lord.*
Jer. 22.15. *Did not thy Father doe Judgment and Justice, and it was well with him?*

Segnius irritant animos demissa per aures,
Quàm quæ sunt oculis commissa fidelibus. *Horat.*
Lege Historiam ne fias Historia. *Cic.*

BOSTON, Printed and Sold by *John Foster* over
against the Sign of the *Dove.* 1 6 7 6.

29. Increase Mather's history of King Philip's War

PHILIP. *KING* of Mount Hope.

32. King Philip, the Wampanoag chieftain who initiated the Indian war of 1675

Hubbard was a Congregational clergyman who desired to 'render a just account of the proceedings' of the people of New England 'together with the merciful providence of the Almighty towards them.' This narrative was the result. Like other early Puritan historians, he described the battles between the Indians and the settlers as a struggle between good and evil.

31   SAMUEL PENHALLOW (1665–1726)

The History of the Wars of New-England, With the Eastern Indians

Boston, 1726. Evans 2796.

Penhallow was a merchant and judge with an interest in history. During the Indian wars from 1702 to 1725, he kept a careful record of events which was published in 1726. He chronicled the 'ghastly deeds' of the Indians, and praised the valor, courage, and righteousness of the people of New England.

32   BENJAMIN CHURCH (1639–1718)

The Entertaining History of King Philip's War

Newport, 1772. Evans 12352.

Benjamin Church played a prominent role in King Philip's War and taught the colonists methods of Indian warfare which they employed successfully to defeat Philip. First published in 1716, Church's history praised the colonists, their courage, and tactics. He argued that the colonists' victory against the Indians and their French allies proved the truth of America's special mission.

This portrait of King Philip was engraved by Paul Revere almost one hundred years after the war. It is a fictitious portrait, based on the eighteenth-century prints of four Indian chiefs by John Simon after paintings by John Verelst.

EDUCATION

From the earliest years of settlement, American colonists valued education highly. They believed that education was necessary for the perpetuation of social, political and religious well-being. Thus as early as 1642 the General Court of Massachusetts Bay decreed that the children of the colony must be educated so that 'learning may not be buried in the graves of our forefathers in Church and Commonwealth.'

By the eighteenth century Americans throughout the colonies had become better able to educate themselves than any other contemporary people. As part of their education, the colonists acquired a familiarity with the classics as well as with contemporary works. The establishment of public and private libraries facilitated the sharing of knowledge and, as Benjamin Franklin later observed, 'made the common tradesmen and farmers as intelligent as most gentlemen from other countries.'

33

The Book of the General Lawes and Libertyes Concerning the Inhabitants of Massachusets

Cambridge, Mass., 1660. Evans 60.

The Puritans believed that Satan kept 'Men from the knowledge of the scripture' and that evil rulers kept men from the knowledge of their rights and liberties. Thus, in 1642 and 1647, the General Court of Massachusetts passed education laws—reprinted in this volume under the heading 'Schools'—which ordered every township with fifty or more householders to provide a teacher, and every town with one hundred householders to provide 'a Grammar school.'

34

The American Primer Enlarged

Philadelphia, [174–?].

This primer is typical of the dozens of primers written for American children. Included in it was an illustrated alphabet, psalms, prayers, the Ten Commandments, other maxims for proper behavior, and proverbs. Education of children was closely allied to the teaching of religious precepts. This unique copy of *The American Primer* was printed in Philadelphia by Andrew Bradford in the early 1740s.

35

A Catalogue of Rare and Valuable Books . . . To Be Sold by Auction

Boston, 1718. Evans 1984.

This early auction catalogue demonstrates the availability and popularity of the Greek and Roman classics plus such modern writers as Descartes, Hobbes, Hutcheson, and Bishop Burnet. The works of colonial writers such as Penn, the Mathers, and others are also listed, as are standard religious works.

36

Catalogus Librorum Bibliothecae Collegij Harvardini

Boston, 1723. Evans 2432.

37

A Catalogue of the Library of Yale-College in New-Haven

New London, 1743. Evans 5320.

These two college library catalogues, the first of each institution, demonstrate the extraordinary interest Americans had in the classics, philosophy, history, natural science, and law. Though religious works are most numerous, the colonists read widely in a variety of fields. They valued their books and their education, for knowledge provided them with a link to the past, legitimized their society, and reinforced their attitudes about their special mission.

38   JAMES LOGAN (1674–1751)

Catalogus Bibliothecae Loganianae

Philadelphia, 1760. Evans 8175.

James Logan was a leading colonial statesman and scholar of Philadelphia. A voracious reader, he collected a library of over three thousand books which he left to the city of Philadelphia. An examination of the catalogue of his library reveals the preponderance of classical works as well as those of Commonwealthmen, Real Whigs, 'radical' Tories, and others opposed to the new financial order in England.

39   MARCUS TULLIUS CICERO

M. T. Cicero's Cato Major, or His Discourse of Old-Age: With Explanatory Notes

Philadelphia, 1744. Evans 5361.

The founder of the Loganian library and internationally recognized as a first-rate botanist, Logan also translated Latin classics into English. Cato symbolized ancient virtue and liberty. Thus John Trenchard and Thomas Gordon, two widely read eighteenth-century English oppositionists, appropriated his name for *Cato's Letters*, a series of attacks on the men and institutions of the Financial Revolution. This copy was presented to Thomas Clap, the president of Yale College, by Benjamin Franklin in 1746.

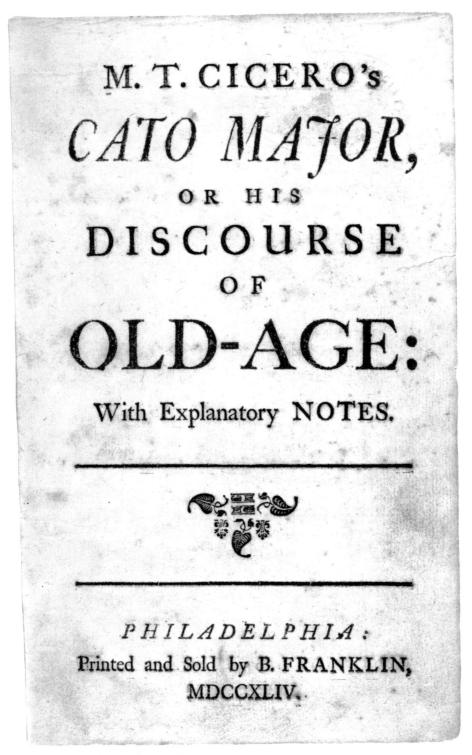

M. T. CICERO's
CATO MAJOR,
OR HIS
DISCOURSE
OF
OLD-AGE:

With Explanatory NOTES.

PHILADELPHIA:
Printed and Sold by B. FRANKLIN,
MDCCXLIV.

39. James Logan's translation of Cicero's *Cato Major*

40

Imported in the Last Ships from London, and to be Sold by David Hall . . .

[Philadelphia, 1754?] Bristol 1649. MP 40686.

This list of books to be sold in Philadelphia is indicative of the books purchased by the colonists. Their interest in history, philosophy, and law is obvious. So too is their fascination with books which instructed them in the fundamentals of carpentry, chemistry, arithmetic, medicine, and trade. They desired to learn and to grow and to become better men as well as to be entertained. Note the availability of Bolingbroke's works in the middle and end of the 'octavo' column, and the emphasis on classics in the schoolbook section.

THE GREAT AWAKENING

During the 1730s and 1740s the growth of towns and the expansion of trade led to the erosion of social and religious order. Concerned ministers and laymen feared that the changes meant that the original principles of the seventeenth-century settlements would be abandoned and that the sense of mission would be lost. Clergymen began to call their flocks to repentance and to warn them of the hell that awaited those who ignored God's commands.

The movement they spawned came to be called the Great Awakening. The message of this new force was that salvation did not result from faithful performance of sacraments and rituals, nor from a life of good works, but simply from opening one's heart to God through prayer. If one sincerely, openly, and unhesitatingly committed oneself to Christ, a profound experience of personal rebirth and salvation would occur. Not only would one's personal soul be saved, but the destiny of America would be preserved as well.

---

41 THEODORUS JACOBUS FRELING-
HUYSEN (1691?–1748)

A Clear Demonstration of a Righteous and Ungodly Man

New York, 1731. Bristol 841. MP 39964.

Frelinghuysen was a Dutch Reformed clergyman, born in Germany, who became a master revivalist. Soon after arriving in New York in 1720 he created a controversy with his new 'emotional' techniques of preaching. He survived many attacks on his evangelism, and along with George Whitefield, Gilbert Tenent, and Jonathan Edwards helped lead the Great Awakening.

42 GEORGE WHITEFIELD (1714–1770)

A Journal of a Voyage from Gibraltar to Georgia

2 vols., Philadelphia, 1740. Bristol 1115. MP 40225 and Evans 4633.

The influence in America of Whitefield, an English evangelist, was far reaching. His arrival in the colonies helped stimulate a religious revival which culminated in the Great Awakening, and which gave great impetus to education, social consciousness, and philanthropic and missionary work. Although others contributed greatly to this movement as well, Whitefield was its most dynamic representative and its unifying element.

THE
DANGER
OF AN
Unconverted Ministry,
CONSIDERED IN A
SERMON
On MARK VI. 34.

By *Gilbert Tennent,* A. M.
And Minister of the Gospel in *New-Brunswick, New-Jersey.*

JEREM. V. 30, 31. *A wonderful and horrible Thing is committed in the Land: The Prophets prophesy falsely, and the Priests bear Rule by their Means, and my People love to have it so; and what will they do in the End thereof?*

From the Second Edition printed at *Philadelphia.*

BOSTON, Printed and Sold by *Rogers* and *Fowle* below the Prison in Queen-Street, near the TOWN-HOUSE. 1742.

45. Gilbert Tennent's sermon on ministers who had not 'seen the light'

43 GEORGE WHITEFIELD (1714–1770)

A Sermon on the Eternity of Hell-Torments

Boston, 1740. Bristol 1120. MP 40229.

This sermon is typical of Whitefield's attacks on an 'earthly minded' clergy and on a populace hanging precipitously over the 'fiery pits of hell.' He admonished everyone to repent and be reborn, and Americans by the thousands were moved to seek such a rebirth.

44 JONATHAN EDWARDS (1703–1758)

Sinners in the Hands of an Angry God

Boston, 1741. Evans 4713.

Edwards, a Congregational clergyman, theologian, and philosopher of Northampton, Massachusetts, was a leader in the first great religious revival of modern times. This famous and pivotal sermon typifies his attempt to intensify the power of Calvinism as a bastion against the secularism of the modern world by fusing original principles of that system with a rapture of mystical communication.

45 GILBERT TENNENT (1703–1764)

The Danger of an Unconverted Ministry, Considered in a Sermon on Mark VI. 34

Boston, 1742. Evans 5070.

Tennent was an immigrant from Ireland who began preaching in Philadelphia as a Presbyterian in 1725. Soon he fell under the influence of Theodorus Frelinghuysen, who encouraged Tennent's natural evangelistic fervor. His sermon *The Danger of an Unconverted Ministry* vividly portrayed the majority of ministers as hypocrites who had the form of godliness but not its power.

LITERATURE

In addition to sharing a general interest in history, the colonists were particularly aware of their own historical role or mission and documented it from an early date. Adventurers described their explorations and discoveries, settlers wrote of Indian wars and captivities, and still others recorded the histories of separate regions or colonies. These histories were often literary manifestations of a nascent American self-consciousness, a realization that American society was unique. It was not yet nationalism, for none of these historians thought of the colonies as a separate nation.

Literature of the seventeenth and eighteenth centuries tended to reflect the Americans' belief in their mission and destiny. Writers persistently praised the abundance and prosperity of the New World, and frequently described the victories of reborn men over nature. Puritan poets in the seventeenth century found such themes especially attractive, as evidenced by the works of Anne Bradstreet, George Herbert, and Michael Wigglesworth. They could also be seen in the eighteenth-century verse of Thomas Godfrey and Nathaniel Evans.

---

46 ROBERT BEVERLEY (1673–1722)

The History of Virginia, in Four Parts

London, 1722.

The second son of one of Virginia's first settlers, Beverley wrote his *History of Virginia* to correct previous barren accounts of the colony's past. This book is an original and shrewd rendering of the foibles of the southern planter, and, unlike other early American books, is written in an unpretentious style.

47 THOMAS PRINCE (1687–1758)

A Chronological History of New-England in the Form of Annals

Boston, 1736. Evans 4068. Gift of Nathaniel Ayer, 1944.

Prince was a theologian, scholar, and bibliophile who received great acclaim as a historian. His *Annals* are lively and discursive, free from the marks of pedantry and propaganda that many of the works of his contemporaries bore. Like other historians of New England, he tended to stress the legitimacy and tradition of New England and the rights and liberties of the inhabitants.

48 JOSEPH BADGER (1708–1765)

Portrait of Thomas Prince (1687–1758)

Oil painting, ca. 1750. Gift of Henry Prentiss, 1836.

The author of *A Chronological History of New England in the Form of Annals*, Prince was a dedicated collector of Americana. He assembled an impressive library in his lifetime, comparable to those of the Mather family and Thomas Hutchinson. Of his fifteen hundred books and tracts, the majority related to the civil and religious history of New England. As an indication of colonial literary taste and as a testimony to the love of learning, the collection, most of which is now housed in the Boston Public Library, is significant.

This portrait was painted by Joseph Badger, the principal portrait artist in Boston between John Smibert and John Singleton Copley. Prince, pastor at Old South Church from 1718 until his death in 1758, is portrayed in clerical robes.

49 PATRICK TAILFER

A True and Historical Narrative of the Colony of Georgia in America

Charleston, S.C., 1741. Evans 4817.

A physician, Tailfer lived in Georgia for a time, but finally settled in South Carolina. In this history he

and his co-authors accused Gen. James Oglethorpe, the founder of Georgia, of selfishness, greed, and despotism. The book was an explicit warning against governors who cared 'not a whit' for the economic welfare of the people. Although this copy bears a Charleston, South Carolina, imprint, it may have been printed in London.

50 JOHN BARTRAM (1699–1777)

Observations on the Inhabitants, Climate, Soil, Rivers . . . Made by Mr. John Bartram in his Travels from Pensilvania to . . . Lake Ontario

London, 1751.

Bartram was America's first native botanist. This journal describes people and weather as well as flora and fauna, and provides an insight into the character of frontier life in colonial America.

51 WILLIAM DOUGLASS (1691?–1752)

A Summary, Historical and Political . . . of the British Settlements in North-America

Boston, 1749–1751. Evans 6307 and 6663.

Douglass was a physician who wrote history. Though marred by inaccuracies, the *Summary* contained a great mass of information on the early colonies. Unlike most colonial historians, Douglass considered the entire North American continent as one geographical and political unit and his book is the first important literary expression of a continental self-consciousness.

52 LEWIS EVANS (ca. 1700–1756)

A General Map of the Middle British Colonies in America

Philadelphia, 1755. Wheat and Brun 298.

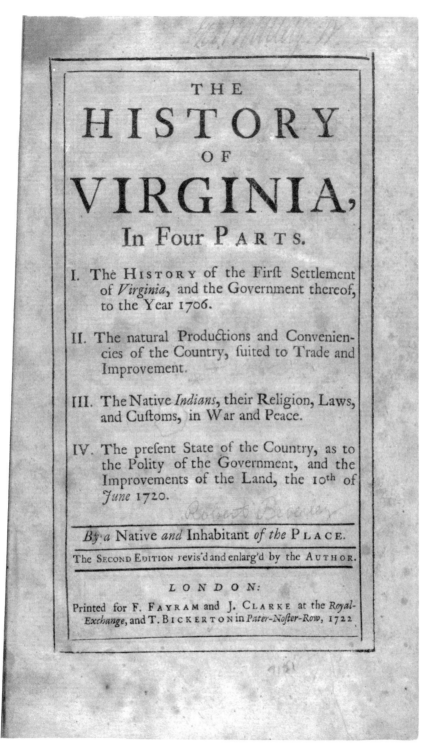

THE
HISTORY
OF
VIRGINIA,
In Four PARTS.

I. The HISTORY of the First Settlement of *Virginia*, and the Government thereof, to the Year 1706.

II. The natural Productions and Conveniencies of the Country, suited to Trade and Improvement.

III. The Native *Indians*, their Religion, Laws, and Customs, in War and Peace.

IV. The present State of the Country, as to the Polity of the Government, and the Improvements of the Land, the 10th of *June* 1720.

By a Native *and* Inhabitant *of the* PLACE.

The SECOND EDITION revis'd and enlarg'd by the AUTHOR.

LONDON:

Printed for F. FAYRAM and J. CLARKE at the *Royal-Exchange,* and T. BICKERTON in *Pater-Noster-Row,* 1722.

46. Robert Beverley's history of Virginia

The compiler of this important American map was Lewis Evans, a geographer and surveyor with a strong interest in the potential value of the Ohio country to the English colonies. This map was regarded as the most detailed and accurate of the region and was reissued many times, the latest being 1814.

53 THOMAS HUTCHINSON (1711–1780)

The History of the Colony of Massachusetts-Bay, from the First Settlement Thereof in 1628

2 vols., Boston, 1764–1767. Evans 9705 and 10658.

Hutchinson was the royal governor of Massachusetts Bay Colony from 1771 to 1774. A member of the colony's elite, and a staunch supporter of the crown and Parliament, Hutchinson became a symbol of British tyranny to the American rebels. Nevertheless, his history remains accurate and informative, and contains documents not available elsewhere. And no one's affection for America or New England was more profound or generous. Unfortunately, he could not separate his love for his country from that for his king. Accordingly, his loyalty cost him everything—his property, home, and country.

54 ANNE BRADSTREET (1612–1672)

Several Poems Compiled with Great Variety of Wit and Learning

Boston, 1678. Evans 244.

Bradstreet came to America in 1630 in Governor Winthrop's party. At first offended by the New World and homesick for England, she later became convinced God had singled America out for some special destiny. She subsequently celebrated New England and America in her poems, and received fulsome accolades from Cotton Mather in his *Magnalia Christi Americana*.

55 THOMAS GODFREY (1736–1763)

Juvenile Poems on Various Subjects

Philadelphia, 1765. Evans 9983.

Godfrey was a poet and playwright, a member of a group of young men in Philadelphia who were among the earliest practitioners of the arts of painting, music, and drama in the colonies. His real claim to remembrance lies in his *Prince of Parthia*, which is contained in this book. *Parthia*, first performed at the Southwark Theater in Philadelphia in 1767, was the first drama written by a native American to be produced upon the professional stage. Godfrey wrote the play for an American company of actors and an American audience.

56 NATHANIEL EVANS (1742–1767)

Poems on Several Occasions, with Some Other Compositions

Philadelphia, 1772. Evans 12386.

Evans was an Episcopal clergyman who made a major contribution to the beginnings of lyric poetry in America. He was one of the Philadelphia group which included Francis Hopkinson and Thomas Godfrey, among others, whose members had high literary ideals and sought to practice those ideals in America. This book was published after his death, and in it one finds a profound celebration of mankind's future.

During the colonial period there were serious economic problems which threatened to destroy the delicate colonial economy and thus society as a whole. Contributing to this threat were the wars fought against the Indians and the French throughout the era, British economic policy, and the lack of gold and silver.

To maintain financial order, without which their mission would fail, colonial leaders insisted on their right to issue paper currency. Currency problems surfaced as early as the 1650s. In the 1760s, colonists perceived British attempts to solve financial problems by regulating colonial money supplies as devious means to tighten imperial control of the colonies.

57 JOHN HULL (1624–1683)

Diary and Memoir

Manuscript.

Hull was the mintmaster and treasurer of the Massachusetts Bay colony, as well as a merchant and silversmith. His diary reveals meticulous business records, orthodoxy and conservatism as a church member, and his important role in the affairs of the colony. In 1652 Massachusetts Bay decided to set up a mint and issue coinage of standard fineness to prevent the circulation of counterfeit coins disruptive to trade. 'They made choice of me for that employment,' wrote Hull. Currency problems would continue to plague New England for generations in spite of Hull's efforts.

58 NATHANIEL HURD (1729–1777)

Coins, Weights, Value

Engraving. Boston, ca. 1750–1760. Gift of Charles H. Taylor, Jr., 1919.

This chart of the internationally accepted weights and values of foreign coins was indispensable to American merchants. Because specie—gold and silver in the form of either coin or bullion—was so quickly drained away to settle commercial imbalances with the mother country, and because the foreign coin that did remain in domestic circulation was often debased and counterfeited, American merchants depended on such charts to insure equitable transactions.

59 JONATHAN DAKIN

Scale for Measuring the Weight of Coins

Boston, ca. 1750–1760.

Used in conjunction with coin valuation charts such as the one glued onto the lid, this scale provided colonial traders with a device to insure the proper value of the scarce specie they received. Jonathan Dakin was a manufacturer of mathematical instruments in Boston in the mid-eighteenth century.

60

Bills of Credit, or Treasury Notes

These bills from New Hampshire (1734), Maryland (1748), and Georgia (1762) are examples of paper currency issued by the various colonial governments in anticipation of future tax receipts. They were issued as a means to supplement the meager money supply in the colonies and thus to facilitate trade. English and American creditors eventually forced Parliament to take action against this 'cheap money' with the Currency acts of 1751 and 1764. To Americans, such parliamentary actions were evidence of a conspiracy against American liberties.

Exchange for £200 Sterl.s N°71 Boston July 27th 1762

Sir

At Thirty days Sight of this my third P Exch.a my first second & fourth of the same Tenor & date unpaid, pay unto John Tyng Esqr or order Two hundred Pounds Sterling, for Value receiv'd, and charge it to the Province of the Massachusetts Bay, but if it is not paid at said thirty Days Sight, then pay Interest on that Sum from the Expiration of said Thirty Days untill paid, at the rate of Six Pounds P C.t P Annum; and if this Bill & Interest is not paid in one Year from the Date hereof, I hereby oblige myself & Successors, in the Office of Treasurer of the Province of the Massachusetts Bay to pay s.d Bill with Interest from the Date of it at the above Rate untill paid, when it shall be Returnd with a Protest into the Office aforesaid, but no other Charges or Damages. Provided, that if Payment be not demanded within Six Months, after the Date of s.d Protest, the Interest shall from that Time Determine & cease.

£200

To

Jasper Mauduit Esq.r Agent for the Province of the Massachusetts Bay in London, or in case of his Death Absence or Refusal of s.d Trust, To Rich.d Jackson jun.r Esq.r

H Gray Prov. Treas.r

61. A bill of exchange, a form of colonial money

61 NATHANIEL HURD (1729–1777)

Bill of Exchange

Boston, 176–.

Bills like this, which was a written order to pay, provided the chief means of transferring funds between the colonies and the mother country. An individual in America, who had a debt to pay in pounds sterling, and had a claim on sterling money, would act as 'drawer.' He would draft the bill and then send it to his creditor in Britain, the 'drawee,' ordering the creditor to hand over a certain sum of money after a stated period of time to a third person, the 'payee.'

62

The Manufactory Scheme . . . Boston, December 4th, 1740

[Boston, 1740.] Bristol 1087. MP 40197.

This is one of several proposals for land banks in the colonies. Such banks were established to circulate paper money in the form of currency issued on loan and secured, or backed by a mortgage. They were designed to increase the money supply and thus aid farmers, merchants, and traders.

63

By His Excellency Jonathan Belcher, Esq; Captain General and Governour in Chief, in and over His Majesty's Province of the Massachusetts Bay in New England. A Proclamation. . . . Boston . . . July 1740

[Boston, 1740.] Bristol 1093. MP 40203.

This proclamation warned the people of Massachusetts about the dangers of bills of credit issued upon a private land bank. Such bills, which facilitated trade and aided independent merchants and traders, were opposed by those who had control of the money supply and good connections with royal officials. Warnings like that contained in the proclamation, however, tended to add impetus to the growing American belief that the British had a malevolent design against American liberties by meddling in the economy.

64

A Letter From a Gentleman in Boston, To His Friend in Connecticut

[Boston, 1744.] Evans 5424.

This pamphlet was written to counter the arguments against bills of credit as raised by a proposed act of Parliament 'to regulate and finally suppress Paper Currencies.' The author reprinted the entire act and then refuted the charges made. He closed his argument with a postscript which asked whether or not the scarcity of gold and silver depreciated colonial money as much as the 'multiplied Emissions of Paper Bills.'

65

To the Honourable the Representatives of the Freemen of the Province of Pennsylvania, in General Assembly Met

[Philadelphia? 176–.] Bristol 2094. MP 41096.

This broadside summed up the problems the colonists had in obtaining a suitable medium of exchange. In it, inhabitants of Chester County, Pennsylvania, gave a brief history of the difficulties, made reference to the Currency Act of 1764, and made an earnest plea to the Pennsylvania General Assembly to emit more bills of credit based on land mortgages in order to relieve the distressed economic situation.

By His EXCELLENCY

JONATHAN BELCHER, Esq;

Captain General and Governour in Chief, in and over His Majesty's Province of the Massachusetts Bay in New England.

A PROCLAMATION.

WHEREAS a Scheme for emitting Bills or Notes by John Colman, Esq; and others, was laid before the Great and General Court or Assembly of this His Majesty's Province, in their Session held at Boston, the Fifth Day of December 1739, and by the Report of a Committee appointed by said Court was represented, if carried on, to have a great Tendency to endamage His Majesty's good Subjects as to their Properties;

And whereas Application has been very lately made to Me and His Majesty's Council, by a great Number of Men of the most considerable Estates and Business, praying that some proper Method may be taken to prevent the Inhabitants of this Province being imposed upon by the said Scheme; and it being very apparent that these Bills or Notes promise nothing of any determinate Value, and cannot have any general, certain or established Credit;

Wherefore,

I Have thought fit, by and with the Advice of His Majesty's Council, to issue this Proclamation, hereby giving Notice and Warning to all His Majesty's good Subjects of the Danger they are in, and cautioning them against receiving or passing the said Notes, as tending to defraud Men of their Substance, and to disturb the Peace and good Order of the People, and to give great Interruption, and bring much Confusion into their Trade and Business.

Given at the Council Chamber in *Boston*, the Seventeenth Day of *July* 1740. In the Fourteenth Year of the Reign of Our Sovereign Lord GEORGE the Second by the Grace of GOD of *Great Britain, France* and *Ireland*, KING Defender of the Faith, &c.

J. BELCHER.

By Order of His Excellency
the Governour, with the
Advice of the Council,
J. Willard, Secr.

GOD save the KING.

WHereas the Committee of the Great and General Court or Assembly at their Sessions begun and held at Boston Dec. 5th 1739, Reported that the Bills proposed to be emitted by John Colman, Esq; and others, would tend to endamage the Properties of His Majesty's good Subjects of this Province; and whereas a large Number of the principal Men of Estates and Business have petitioned His Excellency the Governour and Council to take such Measures as they in their Wisdom should think proper to prevent People's being imposed upon by the said Scheme commonly called the Land Scheme or Bank; whereupon the Governour & Council have issued a Proclamation warning and cautioning People against the said Bills: And we the Subscribers being abundantly perswaded that the said Scheme, if carried on, will be of pernicious Consequence; and being willing and desirous to do what in us lies to prevent the said Imposition, hereby Agree, Declare and Promise, that we will not, directly or indirectly by our selves or any for us, receive or take any Bills emitted on the said Scheme, commonly called the Land Bank. And we hereby caution and advise all Persons whatsoever who are indebted to us, or deal with us, that they refuse the said Bills and do not take any of them in Expectation of our receiving them at their Hands, we being determined not to take the said Bills for any Debts due, nor for any Goods, or on any Consideration whatever.

John Osborne	Thomas Green	Habijah Savage
Edward Hutchinson	John Spooner	Jonathan Armitage
John Alford	Joseph Dowfe	James Allen
Samuel Welles	Robert Temple	William Bolean
Benjamin Lynde	Joseph Brandon	Nathanael Vial
Joshua Winslow	Rufus Green	John Winslow
James Bowdoin	Samuel Demming	John Gibbins
Peter Fanueil	Thomas Palmer	John Tyler
James Smith	Stephen Bouteneau	Nathanael Balston
Charles Apthorp	John Green	William Douglas
John Erving	Benjamin Green	Thomas Austin
Hugh Hall	Byfield Lyde	William Wyer
John Jekyl	Nath Shower	Andrew Hall
Benjamin Fanueil	Benjamin Hallowell	Benjamin Pollard
James Bouteneau	Peter Kenwood	John Trail
John Gooch	Thomas Childs	John Hill
Henry Caswell	Thomas Perkins	Joseph Fitch
Edward Tyng	Charles Paxton	Francis Johonnet
Nath. Cunningham	Samuel Wentworth	Thomas Lambert
William Spikeman	Robert Lightfoot	Joseph Gooch
William Lambert	James Gould	David Le Galley
Andrew Oliver	Ralph Inman	Jeremiah Green
Thomas Oxnard	John Homans	Isaac Gridley
Samuel Sewall	Thomas Lechmere	Benjamin Bagnall
Thomas Gunter	William Winslow	William Lance
Edmund Quincy	Joseph Lee	Josh. Henshaw, jun.
Josiah Quincy	Benjamin Bourn	David Wyar
Joseph Gerrish	Jacob Griggs	James Russell
John Barrel	Richard Clark	Andrew Newell
William Bowdoin	Henry Laughton	Robert Lewis
Francis Boreland	John Cutler	John Minot
John Fayerweather	John Dennie	Samuel Cary
Thomas Hutchinson	John Simpson	John Austin
Thomas Hubbard	Jonathan Simpson	Richard Sutton
Thomas Hancock	James Pitts	John Jones
John Wendell	Stephen Greenleafe	Cornelius Waldo
William Coffin	Joshua Cheever	James Day
Harrison Gray	Thomas Jackson	Thomas Hawden
Timothy Emerson	Samuel Gardner	Henry Withered
Isaac Winslow	Thomas Gardner	John Barret
Joseph Green	Thomas Lee	Norton Quincy
Isaac Walker	Benjamin Clark	Zech. Johonnet
Edward Jackson	Joseph Green	Hopestill Foster
Ebenezer Holmes	John Turner, jun.	John Grant
William Clark	William Tyler	Charles Deming.
William Sheaffe	Samuel Bridgham	

It is hoped, That Masters and Mistresses of Family's will caution their Servants from taking in exchange or otherwise, any of said Bills if offered them, as such a thing may serve to give 'em an entrance into Credit, which would prove of dangerous consequence.

63. Governor Belcher's proclamation against bills of credit and land banks

The French and Indian War, which was fought between 1754 and 1760, was the last and decisive conflict in a worldwide struggle between England and France for dominance and possession of the North American continent. The Battle of Louisbourg in 1745 had primed the Americans for a subsequent struggle. Although the colonists had been victorious, the British returned Louisbourg to the French a few years later. Control of the Ohio Valley was the issue, however, which finally caused the reopening of hostilities. Fighting began when the troops of Virginia under George Washington were fired upon by a detachment of French troops at the junction of the Monongahela and Allegheny rivers.

The first two years were disastrous for the English, but after William Pitt assumed leadership in England,

the tide turned. Louisbourg surrendered to Lord Amherst in July 1758 and the fall of Forts Frontenac and Duquesne followed. In May 1759, the French withdrew from Fort Ticonderoga and Crown Point, and surrendered Fort Niagara in July. The decisive victory for the English was the daring and successful assault on Quebec by General Wolfe in September 1759. On September 8, 1760, after the fall of Montreal, the French signed terms of capitulation which ended the war in America. Final peace came with the Treaty of Paris (1763) by which the French transferred Canada and all its dependencies to the English crown, thus ending a rivalry in North America which had lasted a hundred and fifty years.

66 BENJAMIN GREEN

Journal of Minutes Made in an Expedition against Louisbourg, 1745

Manuscript, French and Indian War Collection.

This journal was apparently written by Benjamin Green, secretary to Sir William Pepperrell, general of the New England troops. Covering the period from March 24 to August 13, 1745, it includes daily entries on the expedition from its inception and departure through its temporary camp at Conso in Nova Scotia, naval engagements, the siege and fall of Louisbourg in June, and the eventual return of the force to New England in the autumn. Though Americans celebrated the victory, and though their feeling of superiority over the French was enhanced, the war disrupted the colonial economy.

67 TIMOTHY CLEMENT

Plan of Hudsons Rivr. from Albany to Fort Edward . . . Lake George, the

Narrows, Crown Point, Part of Lake Champlain with its South Bay and Wood Creek

Boston, 1756. Wheat and Brun 322.

Clement, who was from Haverhill, Massachusetts, drew the map on February 10, 1756. It shows the encampment and major combat zones of the Battle of Lake George. The map is dedicated to William Shirley, the governor of Massachusetts. The campaign to take Crown Point, which precipitated the Battle of Lake George, was led by Sir William Johnson. Though the British commander won great accolades, the British troops were defeated by the French.

68 ASA BURR (1739/40-1816)

Diary, 1758

Manuscript.

This diary, written by a private in Colonel Williams's regiment during the French and Indian War, records

45

67. The Hudson River from Albany to Fort Edward in 1756

the march in May and June 1758 of the Massachusetts militia from Roxbury, Massachusetts, west to Albany and Schenectady, New York. Later diary entries report progress of the British armies on other fronts, but give little real information on the activity of Burr's regiment in the Mohawk Valley. The sparse entries convey a feeling of boredom and routine as well as a vague resentment.

69

On the Landing of the Troops in Boston, September 13th, 1758

[Boston, 1758.] Bristol 1989. MP 40998.

This broadside celebrates the landing of British troops in Boston after the reduction of Fortress Frontenac in Quebec. It is fervently pro-British, and represents one of the last patriotic outbursts for combined Anglo-American enterprises. When British troops next landed in Boston, the reaction of the people, including those who wrote ballads such as this one, was decidedly different.

70

Canada Subjected. A New Song

No place, [1759?]. Bristol 2015. MP 41027.

The topic of this ballad is the successful siege of Montreal which ended the French and Indian War in North America. The woodcut illustration was used on an earlier broadside—Earthquakes Improved—which was printed at Boston in 1755 after an earthquake struck New England. Its use here suggests that this broadside was printed immediately after the news was received without wasting time to make an appropriate illustration for it.

71   MARCUS TULLIUS CICERO

Orationum Marci Tullii Ciceronis

2 vols. Hanover, 1606. Gift of Elizabeth T. Thornton, 1923.

This copy of Cicero's Orations was the property of John Cotton, the Puritan clergyman-settler of Massachusetts Bay. Cicero's philosophy, which expounded virtue and the blessings of agriculture, found a wide audience in colonial America and remained popular for generations as one of the main elements in a classical education.

The American colonists admired earlier, simpler societies, and found that works of classical authors who wrote nostalgically of a golden agrarian past reinforced their ideals. They likewise were avid readers of such seventeenth-century English writers as Sydney, Locke, Milton, and Harrington, who also praised earlier, more virtuous agrarian societies.

Eighteenth-century oppositionists such as Burgh, Trenchard and Gordon, and Bolingbroke continued these themes, and increased the colonists' aversion to Britain's economic system. Bolingbroke developed the ideas of the ancients and British oppositionists into an ideology of resistance, which became in America a 'Gospel of Opposition.' It was this cluster of ideas, derived from earlier political works, that the colonists would repeatedly apply to their own situation respecting England and later their fellow Americans.

72 JAMES HARRINGTON (1611–1677)

The Oceana and Other Works of James Harrington Esq.

London, 1747.

Harrington was a political theorist and the author of the classic statement of Whig political ideals in *The Commonwealth of Oceana* (1656). Other Whigs who followed Harrington's political theories became known as Commonwealthmen. The book sets forth the criteria for an ideal government, including such concepts as separation of powers, rotation in office, and the right of people to remove wicked or unfit governments. Harrington also promoted a 'country ideology' which stressed the importance of owning, living on, and tilling the land and which urged the electorate to choose 'country gentlemen' as their leaders.

73 JOHN MILTON (1605–1674)

The History of Britain

London, 1695.

Milton was not only a great poet (*Paradise Lost*, 1667), but also an effective political pamphleteer. His tracts favoring freedom of the press and divorce stand as landmarks of English political thinking. But it was this history and other Whiggish political tracts, which attacked the crown's prerogative and asked for political reform, that gave him a reputation in America as a friend of liberty.

74 ALGERNON SYDNEY (1622–1683)

Discourses Concerning Government

London, 1704.

A friend and follower of James Harrington, Sydney was a governor of Ireland and republican politician who wrote these essays as an answer to claims of absolute power and royal prerogative made by King Charles II. Sydney was convicted of treason and beheaded in 1683, but his *Discourses Concerning Government*, which upheld the doctrine of the mutual compact and assailed arbitrary and unconstitutional power, became a classic. American colonists often referred to Sydney and his *Discourses* when they spoke of the tyranny of power.

75 JOHN LOCKE (1632–1704)

An Essay Concerning the True Original Extent and End of Civil Government

Boston, 1773. Evans 12834.

THE
OCEANA
AND
OTHER WORKS
OF

James Harrington Esq;

Collected, Methodiz'd, and Review'd,

WITH

An Exact Account of his LIFE

PREFIX'D,

By *JOHN TOLAND.*

To which is added,

An APPENDIX, containing all the Political Tracts wrote by this AUTHOR,

Omitted in Mr. TOLAND's Edition.

RESPUBLICA *Res* eſt *Populi* cum benè ac juſtè geritur, ſive ab uno Rege, ſive a paucis Optimatibus, ſive ab univerſo Populo. Cum vero injuſtus eſt Rex (quem Tyrannum voco) aut injuſti Optimates (quorum Conſenſus Factio eſt) aut injuſtus ipſe Populus (cui nomen uſitatum nullum reperio, niſi ut ipſum Tyrannum appellem) non jam vitioſa ſed omnino nulla Reſpublica eſt, quoniam non RES eſt POPULI cum Tyrannus eam Factióve capeſſat; nec ipſe Populus jam Populus eſt ſi ſit injuſtus, quoniam non eſt Multitudo Juris conſenſu & Utilitatis communione ſociata.

Fragmentum Ciceronis ex lib. 3. de Republica, apud Auguſtin. de Civ. Dei, l. 2. c. 21.

THE THIRD EDITION:
With an ALPHABETICAL INDEX of the Principal Matters.

LONDON:
Printed for A. MILLAR, oppoſite to *Catharine-ſtreet*, in the *Strand.*
M.DCC.XLVII.

72. James Harrington's *Oceana*, the classic statement of Whig political ideals

Locke was an English philosopher who undertook a systematic investigation of the nature of human understanding in order to determine the nature of knowledge. He thus became the founder of epistemology, or the theory of knowledge. This tract postulated that governments existed by virtue of voluntary agreements, or contracts, between the governed and the governors. The government's function was to protect the individual's natural rights to life, liberty, and property. If a government broke such a contract by depriving the people of their natural rights, the people had no recourse but to form a new government and establish a new contract. Locke's ideas were used as an explanation of the Glorious Revolution in England, and they were embraced by the colonists, especially Virginians, and became part of an American ideology of resistance. This is the first American edition of Locke's tract.

76 JOHN LOCKE (1632–1704)

A Letter Concerning Toleration

Boston, 1743. Evans 5227.

This *Letter* was first printed in Latin in 1689; an English translation appeared a year later. The tract is a plea for toleration, but only for Protestant believers, not for Catholics or atheists. As secretary to the Lords Proprietor of Carolina from 1669 to 1672, he drew up the colony's first constitution (never enacted) featuring a highly aristocratic government, slavery, and limited religious freedom.

77 JAMES BURGH (1714–1775)

Britain's Remembrancer

Philadelphia, 1748. Evans 6104.

A mid-eighteenth-century English oppositionist, Burgh had a large following in the colonies. This pamphlet attacked the corruption inherent in the eco-nomic, political, and social systems of contemporary England. The men and institutions of the Financial Revolution were blamed for perverting the constitution. Burgh wrote that only in America, where the new financial order had not penetrated, did the flame of liberty still burn brightly.

78

The Independent Whig

Philadelphia, 1724. Evans 2537.

Edited by two early eighteenth-century English oppositionists, John Trenchard (1662–1723) and Thomas Gordon (d. 1750), *The Independent Whig* exposed the sham, hypocrisy, and power politics of the Anglican hierarchy in England. Trenchard and Gordon were frequently quoted and paraphrased in American political tracts. Together with Henry St. John, Viscount Bolingbroke, they contributed to the creation of an American 'Gospel of Opposition.'

79 HENRY ST. JOHN, VISCOUNT BOLINGBROKE (1678–1751)

Letters, on the Spirit of Patriotism: On the Idea of a Patriot King: and on the State of Parties, at the Accession of King George the First

London, 1750.

Bolingbroke, a statesman and philosopher, led the English opposition movement during the ministry (1721–1742) of Sir Robert Walpole. In 1726 he began to write a series of blistering attacks against Walpole and the new financial order which Walpole had regularized. Bolingbroke used his weekly journal, *The Craftsman*, and such tracts as these to assail the new economic policies. His polemics were widely read in the colonies and were of crucial importance in the formulation of an American 'Gospel of Opposition.'

LETTERS,

ON THE

Spirit of PATRIOTISM:

ON THE

Idea of a PATRIOT KING:

AND

On the STATE of PARTIES,

AT THE

Accession of King GEORGE the First.

LONDON:
Printed for A. MILLAR, opposite to *Catharine-street*, in the *Strand*.
MDCCL.

79. Widely read works of the Tory political theorist Henry St. John, Viscount Bolingbroke

THE
Colonel Dismounted:

OR THE

Rector Vindicated.

In a Letter addressed to His REVERENCE:

CONTAINING

A Dissertation upon the CONSTITUTION *of the* COLONY.

By COMMON SENSE.

Quodcunque ostendis mihi sic, incredulus odi.

HOR.

WILLIAMSBURG:

Printed by JOSEPH ROYLE, MDCCLXIV.

81. Richard Bland's well-stated argument for self-government

The American Revolution

THE FIRST IMPERIAL CRISIS, 1760–1766

As a result of the French and Indian War (called the Seven Years' War in Europe), which ended in 1763, Britain more than doubled the size of her overseas domain. But strains began to be felt in the newly enlarged empire almost as soon as the American phase of the war had ended late in 1759. The sources of strain were varied, but all were related to economic and political disputes which set in motion a destructive process of action and reaction between the colonies and England. At first the disputes were, as in the controversies over the Writs of Assistance and the Parsons' Cause, scattered, local, and seemingly insignificant. They multi-plied rapidly, however, becoming more intense with each passing season.

At the time, British policies were perceived by different Americans in different ways. Land-hungry Pennsylvanians, for example, were most disturbed by the Proclamation of 1763, rum-distilling New Englanders by the Sugar Act, and specie-poor Virginians by the Currency Act. Of all the British actions prior to 1774, only the Stamp Act evoked in the colonies a united front of opposition, and when the act was repealed a wave of euphoria and a sense of accomplishment swept over all the colonies. The first great crisis had passed.

---

80 JAMES OTIS (1725–1783)

The Rights of the British Colonies Asserted and Proved

Boston, 1764. Adams 4a. Evans 9773.

Otis was a statesman, politician, and Revolutionary leader who spoke out against 'Writs of Assistance' (orders giving blanket authority for searches and seizures) as early as 1760. He couched his arguments in such radical language that John Adams, who heard him, wrote years later, 'Then and there was the first act of opposition, to the arbitrary claims of Great Britain. Then and there, the child independence was born.' This pamphlet continued Otis's assertions that the Americans were not bound to obey laws that they had had no part in making. He added that in all questions relating to the expenditure of public money the rights of a colonial legislature were as sacred as the rights of Parliament.

81 RICHARD BLAND (1710–1776)

The Colonel Dismounted: Or the Rector Vindicated

Williamsburg, 1764. Adams 1. Bristol 2457. MP 41432.

Bland was a member of the Virginia House of Burgesses. It is likely that he wrote both of the 'Two Penny' bills, which were enactments designed to raise revenue for the colony of Virginia during the French and Indian War. In this pamphlet he supported the right of the General Assembly to enact this legislation, which provided for a reduction of the salaries of the Anglican clergy. He also supported Patrick Henry during the famous 'Parsons' Cause' controversy. Such attitudes presaged his bitter attack on the British financial system in *An Inquiry into the Rights of the British Colonies* (1766).

53

82

. . . An Act for Granting Certain Duties . . . for Continuing, Amending, and Making Perpetual, an Act . . . (Intituled, An Act for the Better Securing and Encouraging the Trade of His Majesty's Sugar Colonies in America)

Boston, 1764. Evans 9682.

Known as the Sugar Act, this measure modified the Molasses Act of 1733 by reducing the duty on molasses imported into America from sixpence to threepence a gallon. The old duty had been designed to regulate trade rather than to provide a revenue. The new reduced duty was designed to increase trade and produce a revenue, but it was still high enough to be virtually ruinous, and merchants were prepared to flout it by smuggling. The new act, however, changed the procedures for collecting so that customs officials personally profited. As a result, officials often ruthlessly enforced the act. The economy of New England suffered accordingly, for molasses used to distill rum was the key to New England's trade.

83

Reasons Against the Renewal of the Sugar Act

Boston, 1764. Adams 6. Evans 9812. Gift of Thomas Wallcut, 1834.

This anonymous pamphlet is typical of dozens written to protest the Sugar Act of 1764. Such tracts argued that the new act had been designed to raise revenue, not regulate trade, and thus amounted to a form of taxation without representation. New Englanders also opposed the act because it restricted the trade of a vital staple. As a result, the colonists began to believe that their economic troubles grew directly out of a consistent set of new policies emanating from England that, taken together, amounted to a deliberate design to oppress them.

84 THOMAS FITCH (1700–1774)

Reasons Why the British Colonies, in America, Should Not Be Charged with Internal Taxes

New Haven, 1764. Adams 3. Evans 9658.

Fitch was the colonial governor of Connecticut, which, like Rhode Island, elected its governors from the membership of the legislature. When, at the end of the Seven Years' War (1756–1763), proposals were first made for parliamentary taxation of the colonies, the Connecticut Assembly requested Fitch and others to draw up the objections of the colony to such legislation. The result was this pamphlet, which was a clear and concise statement of the constitutional, historical, and economic arguments of the colony against the proposed stamp tax.

85

Martis, 29 Die Octobris, A.D. 1765. In the House of Representatives

[Boston, 1765.] Evans 10065.

This broadside contains a list of resolves made by the House of Representatives for the colony of Massachusetts only a few days before the Stamp Act was implemented. The resolves pertain primarily to the rights and liberties of the colonists and assert that Americans are entitled to the same protection as Englishmen anywhere. Resolutions eleven and twelve discuss the Royal Charter and point out that, according to the original principles of the colony, only the General Court of Massachusetts could levy taxes on the colonists. Resolution thirteen refers to the admiralty courts set up by the Sugar Act of 1764 and asserts that such courts are unconstitutional.

86

. . . An Act for Granting and Applying Certain Stamp Duties

London, 1765.

REASONS

WHY

The *BRITISH* COLONIES,

IN

AMERICA,

SHOULD NOT BE CHARGED WITH

INTERNAL TAXES,

BY AUTHORITY OF

PARLIAMENT;

HUMBLY OFFERED,

For CONSIDERATION,

In Behalf of the COLONY of

CONNECTICUT.

NEW-HAVEN:
Printed by B. MECOM. M,DCC,LXIV.

84. Thomas Fitch's pamphlet against British taxes

This act required the use of tax stamps which cost from threepence to several pounds on most printed materials, including newspapers. The storm of protest which resulted in the colonies led to the Stamp Act Congress, the Committees of Correspondence, the Sons of Liberty, and the conviction that a conspiracy existed in London to deliberately deprive the colonists of their liberties.

87 DANIEL DULANY (1722–1797)

Considerations on the Propriety of Imposing Taxes in the British Colones [sic]

New York, 1765. Adams 11c. Evans 9958.

Dulany, a Maryland lawyer and politician, published this pamphlet eight months after the passage of the Stamp Act. The essay contended that the colonists were not and could not be represented in Parliament, and that taxation without representation was a violation of the constitution of England. He maintained that the colonists should develop their own industries and thus remove the chance of being economically oppressed. William Pitt freely drew upon Dulany's arguments when speaking for repeal of the Stamp Act in Parliament. Ironically, when war arrived Dulany became a loyalist.

88

The Last Shift

Engraving, [London, 1765]. British Museum Catalogue 4118.

This engraving, apparently a book illustration, depicts the attempt to tax the American colonies by the Stamp Act of 1765. An official of the English government presenting a brace of pistols to a party of gentlemen cries, 'Stand and deliver.' They reply, 'We are all Americans.' Lord Bute in the background tells the king to follow his minister's instructions and all would go well. The king says, 'Necessity Pinches me, Money we must have.'

89

The State of the Nation An: Dom: 1765 &c.

Engraving, [London, 1765]. British Museum Catalogue 4130.

Dissension in the British government over the Stamp Act is the focus of this anonymous etching. Britannia, leaning her head on the shoulder of an angry America, is in distress. George Grenville, chancellor of the exchequer and first lord of the treasury, who promoted the Stamp Act, rushes forward with his sword drawn, crying that he will enforce the act. He is stopped by William Pitt (holding the spear and cap of Liberty) who declares, 'You have no right.' On the other side, Lord Mansfield, who is acting under the directions of Lord Bute, wants to assail Britannia, but is stopped by Lord Camden, a friend of America, who insists on there being 'no general warrants,' such as were used against John Wilkes. In the distance, two large ships, English and American, are driving onto a rocky shore.

90 PAUL REVERE (1735–1818)

A View of the Year 1765

Engraving, Boston, [1766]. Stauffer 2694.

This engraving by Revere depicts the Stamp Act as a dragon confronting 'Boston' with a drawn sword. The other figures supporting the stand of the city are identified by the text of the print. At the right hangs John Huske, who had become a member of Parliament after leaving his native New Hampshire and who allegedly supported the Stamp Act. He was hanged in effigy from the Liberty Tree on November 1, 1765. Also commemorated is the outbreak of August 14, 1765, when Andrew Oliver, the stampmaster, was hanged in effigy. Revere copied this engraving from an English print, 'View of the Present Crisis,' which was published in April 1763.

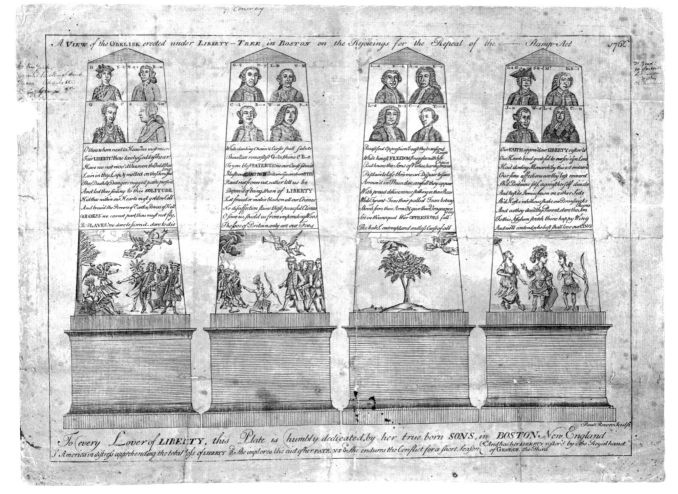

93. Paul Revere's engraving of the obelisk built to celebrate the repeal of the Stamp Act

91

The Examination of Doctor Benjamin Franklin, before an August Assembly, Relating to the Repeal of the Stamp-Act, &c.

Philadelphia, 1766. Adams 31. Evans 10300.

Before Parliament would repeal the Stamp Act, it felt obliged to assert its supremacy. Franklin gave Parliament a way to save face, although in doing so, he confused the issues and guaranteed future misunderstandings. In testifying before Parliament, Franklin explained that Americans distinguished between external and internal taxation, approving of the former, and disapproving of the latter. Franklin hinted that if Parliament repealed the Stamp Act, firmly asserted its authority, and drafted legislation more carefully in the future, the colonies would comply with future legislation. Parliament, persuaded by this line of reasoning, repealed the Stamp Act on March 18, 1766, and passed the Declaratory Act which stated that Parliament had full power to enact laws binding the colonies.

92

Glorious News. Boston, Friday 11 o'Clock, 16th May 1766

[Boston, 1766.] Evans 10317.

The colonists greeted the repeal of the Stamp Act in 1766 with general rejoicing. This broadside, which describes the repeal and the celebration in London, reveals that the English merchants as well as the Americans were relieved by 'the great, glorious and important News.'

93   PAUL REVERE (1735–1818)

A View of the Obelisk Erected under Liberty-Tree in Boston

Engraving, [Boston, 1766]. Stauffer 2695. Bequest of Mary L. Eliot, 1927.

To help celebrate the repeal of the Stamp Act, Bostonians erected an obelisk which showed the king and queen of England as well as fourteen English patriots and an allegorical representation of America's struggle for liberty. The obelisk was used for setting off fireworks which subsequently destroyed it. Fortunately, Paul Revere had engraved this view of the obelisk before its destruction. The engraving is among the scarcest of Revere's prints, only two copies being known.

A second imperial crisis quickly followed the first. Although British leaders had misunderstood the opposition to the stamp tax, and abandoned the effort to impose internal taxes on the colonies, they were still determined that British Americans should help bear the cost of their own defense. Accordingly, in 1767 Britain imposed various external taxes in the form of import duties, and expected the colonists to pay quietly. The Americans were startled and felt that they had been betrayed. Once again they resisted. The British were equally startled by the American response and they too felt betrayed.

At each point of this new crisis colonists and Britons demanded explanations and attempted to define, explain, and justify their own positions. But every new definition of position by one party engendered suspicion and distrust in the other, until by 1770 the crisis reached such extreme proportions that myopia began to give way to a far deadlier disorder, paranoia. Such events as the Boston Massacre strengthened that condition considerably.

94

At a Meeting of Freeholders and Other Inhabitants of the Town of Boston . . .

[Boston, 1767.] Evans 10564.

This broadside spells out clearly the economic problems which confronted the colonists in 1767 as a result of the French and Indian War, the lack of a circulating medium, and the recently passed taxes and duties of the Townshend Acts. It asked that the colonists refrain from importing a variety of articles from abroad, and attacked foreign 'Superfluities.' A concerted effort at nonimportation was urged so that local industry might be promoted.

95 JOHN DICKINSON (1732–1808)

Letters from a Farmer in Pennsylvania to the Inhabitants of the British Colonies

Pennsylvania Chronicle, December 2, 1767 – February 15, 1768.

Dickinson was a Pennsylvania lawyer with a strong interest in history and politics. In 1765 he published a pamphlet, *The Late Regulations Respecting the British Colonies . . . Considered,* which stated that the only way to secure the repeal of the Sugar and Stamp Acts was to enlist English merchants on the American side by appealing to their economic interest. Largely because of this pamphlet he became one of Pennsylvania's delegates to the Stamp Act Congress at New York. In December 1767, he began publishing pseudonymously in the *Pennsylvania Chronicle* a series of essays beginning with this one, signed 'A Farmer.' In these articulate letters he pointed out the evils of the British policy, suggested force as an ultimate remedy, but stated a belief that reconciliation was possible. The *Letters,* although pacific in tone, showed wide knowledge both of practical economics and of the broad legal principles underlying English liberty and became, with Thomas Paine's later pamphlets, the most influential publications leading to revolution.

96 SAMUEL ADAMS (1722–1803)

'A Puritan'

Boston Gazette, and Country Journal, April 18, 1768.

Adams was one of the founders of the Sons of Liberty in Massachusetts and a fiery patriot from the early

1760s. He was probably more influential than any other person in inciting the hatred toward the British troops which culminated in the Boston Massacre. His influence was due not only to his unrivalled skill as a local politician, but also to his abilities as a polemical writer. Such letters as this one, signed 'A Puritan,' for example, analyzed specific problems of the British political, economic, and religious systems. Adams implicitly asserted that Americans were entitled to the rights and liberties of Englishmen, that Parliament had no authority over the colonies, and that a revolution would occur if England continued to force its policies on America.

97 SILAS DOWNER (1729–1785)

A Discourse, Delivered in Providence . . . the 25th. Day of July, 1768. At the Dedication of the Tree of Liberty . . .

Providence, 1768. Adams 55. Evans 10886.

Downer was a Providence lawyer who was secretary of the local Committee of Correspondence, a member of the town committee to draft instructions to the representatives to oppose the Stamp Act, and a member of the Sons of Liberty. In this pamphlet he painted an idyllic picture of American life under the old economic system, and denied that England had ever provided America any benefits. He believed that England had been attempting to place the colonies in economic bondage, and he cried 'Tyranny!'

98

An Elegy to the Infamous Memory of Sr. F[rancis] B[ernard]

[Boston], 1769. Evans 11246.

This poem attacked Sir Francis Bernard, who had just completed nine stormy years as royal governor of Massachusetts. During his tenure, the Sugar and Stamp Acts were passed, the hated Writs of Assistance were issued, and troops were quartered in Boston. The cut of the segmented snake first appeared in

The Constitutional Courant for September 21, 1765 (Woodbridge, N.J.: Andrew Marvel) and was reprinted in New York, Boston, and Philadelphia. This is apparently its first appearance in a pamphlet.

99

The Following Patriotic Toasts were Drank on the 19th Instant . . .

[New York, 1770.] Unrecorded.

In New York, as in other colonies, the repeal of the Stamp Act was commemorated annually. The New York celebration of 1770 was, however, different from previous years. The patriots split into two groups. This broadside records the toasts of the more radical group. The twentieth toast was the most significant since the other group, the Sons of Liberty and Trade, felt that trade was being sacrificed unduly in the zeal for liberty.

100

A Particular Account of the Most Barbarous and Horrid Massacre!

[Boston? 1770.] Bristol 3241. MP 42145.

Tensions in Boston during the winter of 1769–1770 had increased steadily. From December on, fights between civilians and soldiers, on and off duty, were almost daily occurrences. Then on March 5, 1770, after a bloody fistfight between a soldier and a worker had sent tempers soaring, bands of civilians and soldiers roamed the town spoiling for a fight. About nine in the evening one of these bands headed for the customs house on King Street. When the sentry spotted it, he hastily called the main guard. As John Adams described the ensuing scene, 'the multitude was shouting . . . and threatening life. The people from all quarters [were] throwing every species of rubbish they could pick up. . . .' Hundreds of reinforcements poured in from neighboring towns to join the mob. The troops restrained themselves until one of them was hit by a brick, whereupon in anger

The following PATRIOTIC

TOASTS

were drank on the 19th Inftant, at Hampton-Hall, by a very numerous Company of the SONS OF LIBERTY in this City, convened at that Place to celebrate the Anniverfary of the Repeal of the STAMP-ACT.

1. MAY the American Colonies fully enjoy the Britifh Conftitution.

2. The KING, as the Head and Preferver of the Conftitution.

3. The QUEEN, Prince of WALES, and all the Royal Family.

4. The Right Honourable the Earl of Dunmore, and the Province.

5. Great-Britain and her Colonies.

6. The fpirited Houfe of Burgeffes in Virginia, in 1765 and 1769.

7. The Ninety-two patriotic Non-Refcinders of the Maffachufetts.

8. The Affemblies on the Continent, that have nobly refufed to comply with the Mutiny Act.

9. All the Friends in America, in Great-Britain, Ireland, and the Colonies.

10. May a Conftitutional Union ever exift between Great-Britain and her Colonies.

11. May the illuftrious Houfe of Hanover, never want a Proteftant Heir to rule the Britifh Empire.

12. May the Defigns of the Enemies of the Britifh Empire, ever be defeated.

13. The immortal Memory of William the Third, and the glorious Revolution.

14. Unanimity to the Colonies to the lateft Pofterity.

15. The LIBERTY of the PRESS.

16. John Wilkes, Efq; for his noble Struggles in the Caufe of Liberty.

17. Captain Alexander MacDOUGAL, who has nobly ftood forth in its Defence.

18. The Freedom of Elections.

19. The Supporters of the Bill of Rights.

20. A Continuance of the Non-Importation Agreement, until the Revenue Acts are repealed.

21. Profperity to the Trade and Manufactories of America.

22. Unanimity among all the Sons of Liberty in America, and Perfeverance in the glorious Caufe.

23. The Navy and Army.

24. Lord Chatham.

25. Lord Cambden.

26. General Conway.

27. Colonel Barre.

28. The prefent patriotic Lord Mayor of London.

29. Mr. Burke.

30. General PAOLI.

31. The Pennfylvania FARMER.

32. The Memory of John Hampden, Efq;

33. The Memory of Algernon Sidney, Efq;

34. Doctor Lucas, the Patriot of Ireland.

35. All the Sufferers for the Caufe of Liberty.

36. The celebrated Female Hiftorian Mrs. M'Auley.

37. The Memory of Andrew Hamilton, Efq; who undauntedly advocated the Caufe of John Peter Zenger.

38. Zenger's Jury, who regardlefs of the Directions of the Court, refufed to bring in a fpecial Verdict, and acquitted the Prifoner.

39. A total Abolition of the Star-Chamber Doctrine of Libels, as held upon the Trials of Zenger, Mead and Penn.

40. Confufion to all Informers, but fuch as contribute to the Salvation of their Country.

41. More public Virtue and Integrity, and lefs Venality throughout the Britifh Empire.

42. The Memory of the Scotch Barons, in the Reign Robert the Firft.

43. The Memory of our late worthy Governor Sir HENRY MOORE.

44. The Committees for infpecting the Non-Importation Agreements in all the Colonies.

45. THE DAY.

99. A commemoration of the repeal of the Stamp Act in New York

and confusion he fired directly into the crowd. In panic, most of the other soldiers also opened fire. When the shooting was over five civilians lay dead. This broadside describes the colonists' version of the 'Massacre.'

101 HENRY PELHAM (1748–1806)

The Fruits of Arbitrary Power, Or the Bloody Massacre

Etching, [Boston, 1770].

This depiction of the Boston Massacre by Henry Pelham was plagiarized by Paul Revere and published under the title of 'The Bloody Massacre perpetrated in King Street.' Both versions, as pieces of propaganda, achieved their aim, but the renderings are inaccurate. The British soldiers did not line up and fire in this manner. The trial of the soldiers, defended by American lawyers including John Adams, found only two of the soldiers guilty of manslaughter. The six others were acquitted.

Henry Pelham, who, like his half-brother John Singleton Copley, became a loyalist and fled to England in 1775, described Revere's plagiarism as 'one of the most dishonorable Actions you could well be guilty of.'

102

A Monumental Inscription on the Fifth of March

[Boston, 1772.] Evans 12302.

The Boston Massacre was commemorated in broadsides as well as in sermons during the Revolutionary period. This piece refers to the Massacre and inveighs against the release of Ebenezer Richardson from jail. Richardson was a despised customs official who had killed Christopher Seider on February 22, 1770, while a mob was gathered outside his door. Tried for manslaughter, pronounced guilty, but never sentenced, Richardson was released from prison on March 10, 1772. The woodcut of the Boston Massacre was engraved by Paul Revere and was first used in Isaiah Thomas's *The Massachusetts Calander* for 1772.

BRITISH SUPPORTERS OF THE AMERICAN CAUSE

During the years of imperial crises the colonists had many friends and supporters in England. Men like John Wilkes, for example, openly advocated American resistance. The colonists believed that the harassment Wilkes had received, including the denial of his seat in the House of Commons to which he had been duly elected, proved that Parliament had clearly become unrepresentative, corrupt, and tyrannical.

Many Americans had an identity of interest with Wilkes and other English radicals. Both groups of oppositionists insisted on their ancient constitutional rights, desired the implementation and preservation of a system of government based on agrarian interests, and opposed governments of power-mad money men. That so many Englishmen sympathized and identified with the cause aided the colonists significantly, for such support powerfully reinforced the basic understanding Americans had of their 'oppression.'

---

103 JOHN WILKES (1727–1797)

The North Briton

London, 1762–1763.

Wilkes, a member of Parliament and a leader of the opposition movement in the 1760s, became a popular hero in Great Britain and in the American colonies. In 1762 he founded *The North Briton*, which, in the guise of a Scottish Tory periodical, attacked the prime minister, Lord Bute, and satirized the government. In 1763 the famous issue No. 45 virtually called George III a liar. Wilkes was thrown into the Tower of London. Released on a writ of habeas corpus, soon he was arrested for seditious libel. Fearing life imprisonment, he fled to Paris, for which flight he was outlawed. He returned to England in 1768 after having been reelected to Parliament. Expelled from Parliament, reelected and expelled again, finally he took his seat in 1774.

104

An Authentick Account of the Proceedings against John Wilkes, Esq.

Philadelphia, 1763. Evans 9542.

The American interest in the Wilkes affair is indicated by the reprinting of 'The North Briton, No. 45' and other documents pertaining to the British oppositionist.

105 BENJAMIN WEST (1730–1813)

Bickerstaff's Boston Almanack, for the Year of Our Lord 1769

Boston, [1768]. Evans 11112.

John Wilkes, the 'Patron of Liberty,' graces the cover of this almanac. On one side of him is Britannia dressed as Minerva, the goddess of wisdom, and on the other is Hercules, the god of strength. Cupid is shown holding aloft a liberty cap. Underneath is a serpent, the emblem of envy, upon which Hercules is treading. 'Lockes Works' and 'Sidney on Government' are also shown because of their well-known association with liberty. Most colonists understood the references completely and considered Wilkes a living symbol of liberty. Benjamin West, the compiler, was an astronomer from Massachusetts who revived the name Isaac Bickerstaff, originated in 1707 in England by Jonathan Swift. He issued almanacs under that name from 1768 through 1779. Frequently containing topical illustrations, the Bickerstaff almanacs appealed to patriots and gained a wide circulation throughout America.

106 PETER PELHAM (ca. 1697–1751)

Portrait of Thomas Hollis (1720–1774)

Mezzotint, Boston, 1751. Stauffer 2466.

Thomas Hollis of London was an ardent supporter of liberty and the constitution. He described himself as 'an Englishman, a lover of liberty, his Country, and its excellent Constitution.' He devoted himself to collecting works of art and books which promoted the theme of liberty or England's ancient Saxon principles. He donated much of what he collected to Harvard College, and became the largest contributor to that institution's library. Among his friends and correspondents in America were Jonathan Mayhew, Edmund Quincy, and Benjamin Franklin.

107 THOMAS POWNALL (1722–1805)

The Administration of the Colonies

London, 1766. Adams 5c.

More than any other Englishman of his time, Pownall deserves to be called a student of colonial administration. As lieutenant governor of New Jersey from 1753 to 1757 and governor of Massachusetts from 1757 to 1760, he labored to drive the French from North America. This book, originally published in 1765, projected the union of all the American possessions in one dominion, and drew attention to the reluctance of colonists to be taxed without their consent. He also wrote of the colonists' allegiance to liberty and virtue and of America's glorious future.

108

The Scourge Numb. I.

Boston, 1771. Evans 12222.

105. A tribute to John Wilkes in *Bickerstaff's Boston Almanack*

This broadside, derived from a London imprint, and issued by Isaiah Thomas, is typical of the English literature sympathetic to the American cause which found its way to the colonies. It describes the current 'corrupt and depraved' condition of the English political and economic system and lists specific instances whereby original constitutional principles had been subverted. The principles upon which a just government stands are listed. 'The Scourge' concludes with the ringing assertion that 'When these principles are violated, and the rights of the people invaded, such violations, and such invasions should be immediately resisted.' Such broadsides encouraged the colonists to believe that only in America did the torch of liberty still burn bright.

109

The Colossus of the North, or The Striding Boreas

Engraving, [London, December 1, 1774]. British Museum Catalogue 5242.

In this cartoon, Lord North stands astride a stream of corruption filled with members of Parliament. John Wilkes tries to stem the stream with a broom as Britannia laments that she has been destroyed by those who should preserve her. The torch labelled America smolders and is one of North's trophies. This print, published in the December 1774 issue of the *London Magazine*, expresses the criticism heaped upon the English government by Englishmen, not just the colonists, and graphically depicts the corruption despised by political theorists on both sides of the water.

110   JAMES BURGH (1714–1775)

Political Disquisitions

2 vols., Philadelphia, 1775. Evans 13851.

Burgh was an English oppositionist whose pamphlets were widely read in America. He lamented the dissolution of English liberties and original principles,

and he blamed the men and institutions of the new financial order. He argued passionately for a restoration of the ancient Saxon constitution, and asserted that only in America did liberty and virtue still reign supreme. He, Bolingbroke, Trenchard, and Gordon contributed greatly to the formation of an American 'Gospel of Opposition.'

111   WILLIAM PITT, FIRST EARL OF CHATHAM (1708–1778)

The Speech of the Right Honourable The Earl of Chatham in the House of Lords, January 20th, 1775

Philadelphia, 1775. Adams 190e. Evans 14405.

Pitt served Great Britain variously as a member of the House of Commons, prime minister, and member of the House of Lords. A supporter of the colonies and their causes, he argued against most of the parliamentary acts designed to raise revenue in America. He implored the ministers to adopt a more gentle mode of governing America, and asserted that England 'had no right under heaven' to tax the colonists. This speech asked the king to recall the troops from Boston, and fully justified the resistance of the Americans. His motion was overwhelmingly defeated.

112   EDMUND BURKE (1729–1797)

The Speech of Edmund Burke, Esquire, On Moving His Resolutions for Conciliation With the Colonies, March 22nd, 1775

New York, 1775. Adams 157e. Evans 13854.

Burke was an orator, political theorist, and member of Parliament who openly sympathized with the American cause. He was for justice and liberty, but unalterably opposed to 'the tyranny of unprincipled ability divorced from religious awe and all regard for individual liberty and property.' Hence the same man who gave this magnificent speech on conciliation with

POLITICAL

DISQUISITIONS;

OR,

An ENQUIRY into public ERRORS, DEFECTS,
and ABUSES. Illuftrated by, and eftablifhed upon
FACTS and REMARKS, extracted from a Variety
of AUTHORS, Ancient and Modern.

CALCULATED

To draw the timely ATTENTION of GOVERNMENT
and PEOPLE, to a due Confideration of the
Neceffity, and the Means, of REFORM-
ING thofe ERRORS, DEFECTS, and
ABUSES; of RESTORING the
CONSTITUTION, and SAV-
ING the STATE.

By J. BURGH, GENTLEMAN; Author of the DIGNITY of
HUMAN NATURE, and other Works.

VOLUME THE FIRST.

PHILADELPHIA:

Printed and Sold by ROBERT BELL, in *Third-Street*; and
WILLIAM WOODHOUSE, in *Front-Street*.

M,DCC,LXXV.

110. James Burgh's highly influential *Political Disquisitions*

113. England trying to control her 'incorrigible' colonies

America later conducted a fierce crusade against the French Revolution.

113

Poor Old England Endeavoring to Reclaim his Wicked American Children

[London], April 1, 1777. British Museum Catalogue 5397.

The publisher of this print, Matthew Darly, issued biting political and social caricatures over a long period. England is represented by an elderly, lame, and emaciated man who attempts to regain control of his colonies by pulling cords attached to hooks in their noses. The attempt is obviously unsuccessful and the colonies, represented by raucous men, tease and taunt England.

THE CLERGY AND RESISTANCE

The New England clergy were a major source of resistance to British policies during the imperial crisis. In election sermons and other orations, they attacked the subversion of American 'Rights, Liberties, and Privileges.' The clergy particularly feared the extension of the Anglican episcopacy into the American colonies, for they considered such change to be a prelude to the transference of the rest of England's corrupt financial and political system to the colonies and a threat to America's mission. Thus they believed that resistance to British designs would not only provide a means to escape the worst aspects of the new social and economic order of England, but would also purify and revitalize the colonies.

114 VALENTINE GREEN (1739–1813)

Portrait of Samuel Cooper (1725–1783)

Mezzotint, London, 1784.

115 SAMUEL COOPER (1725–1783)

The Crisis

[Boston], 1754. Evans 7176.

Cooper was a Boston clergyman who was active early in the cause of American freedom and intimately associated with its leaders. In 1754 he published this pamphlet anonymously against a government excise and the extension of the British financial system to America. Moreover, before and during the Revolution, he was a frequent contributor to the newspapers and an orator on the popular side. This portrait, a mezzotint engraving, represents the typical clergyman of the period, in wig, gown, and bands. It was copied after a painting owned by John Hancock.

116 JONATHAN MAYHEW (1720–1766)

The Snare Broken. A Thanksgiving-Discourse

Boston, 1766. Adams 35a. Evans 10388.

Frequently called the founder of American Unitarianism, Mayhew was steeped in the Commonwealthman literature of Locke, Sidney, Milton, and Harrington. Among his friends, he included James Otis, Josiah Quincy, and Samuel Adams, all fervent patriots. He preached many 'radical' sermons, some of the most famous of which attacked the Society for the Propagation of the Gospel, an organization he viewed as a front for the establishment of an episcopacy in America. Mayhew's most famous sermon, however, was *The Snare Broken*. In it he attacked Britain for 'sucking the lifeblood' out of America by means of a series of calculated economic measures and acts.

REMARKS
ON AN ANON·TRACT
P·LXXXII

IONATHAN MAYHEW, D·D·PASTOR OF THE WEST CHVRCH
IN BOSTON, IN NEW ENGLAND, AN ASSERTOR OF THE CIVIL
AND RELIGIOVS LIBERTIES OF HIS COVNTRY AND MANKIND,
WHO, OVERPLIED BY PVBLIC ENERGIES, DIED OF A NERVOVS FEVER,
IVLY VIIII, MDCCLXVI, AGED XXXXV

I·B·CIPRIANI   MDCCLXVII·

117. Jonathan Mayhew, a leader of the American resistance movement

A

DISCOURSE

On " the good News from
a far Country."

Deliver'd *July* 24*th*.

A Day of Thanks-giving to Almighty GOD,
throughout the Province of the *Maſſachuſetts-
Bay* in *New-England*, on Occaſion of the
REPEAL of the STAMP-ACT ; appointed
by his Excellency, the GOVERNOR of ſaid
Province, at the Deſire of it's Houſe of RE-
PRESENTATIVES, with the Advice of his
MAJESTY'S COUNCIL.

By CHARLES CHAUNCY, D.D.
A Paſtor of the firſt Church in *Boſton*.

BOSTON: N.E.

Printed by KNEELAND and ADAMS, in Milk-ſtreet,
for THOMAS LEVERETT, in Corn-hill.

MDCCLXVI.

118. Charles Chauncy's biting sermon against an episcopacy in America

117 GIOVANNI BAPTISTA CIPRIANI (1727–1785)

Portrait of Jonathan Mayhew (1720–1766)

Etching, London, 1767.

Mayhew, a liberal Boston clergyman, was a leading figure in the formation of the ideology of the American Revolution. His most influential sermons were those preached against the 'papist' doctrines of the Church of England. This likeness portrayed Mayhew as a lover of liberty and enemy of priestcraft (note the bishop's mitre with a viper in it, tied to the wreath of liberty). The etching was executed by Giovanni Cipriani, an Italian artist who was commissioned frequently by Thomas Hollis to portray men of liberty.

118 CHARLES CHAUNCY (1705–1787)

A Discourse on 'the Good News from a Far Country'

Boston, 1766. Adams 24. Evans 10255.

Chauncy was one of the most influential clergymen in New England. He wrote many pamphlets and sermons attacking the establishment of an episcopacy in America. He condemned those who needed a church hierarchy and asserted that it ought to be 'left to the wisdom of particular communities to determine what form of government shall take place among them.' He also accused the English of becoming 'papist degenerates.'

119 SAMUEL COOKE (1709–1783)

A Sermon Preached at Cambridge in the Audience of His Honor Thomas Hutchinson, Esq.

Boston, 1770. Evans 11613.

Cooke was the minister of the First Congregational Church of Arlington, Massachusetts. His sermons during the early 1770s were bitter attacks against the unconstitutional policies of the British. He associated Governor Hutchinson with all the 'evils and corruptions' he believed existed in England, and called the redcoats 'Hutchinson's Butchers.' This sermon discusses the origin and nature of government, the constitutional history of Massachusetts, and the nature of the tie with the empire.

120 SAMUEL LANGDON (1723–1797)

Government Corrupted by Vice, and Recovered by Righteousness

Watertown, 1775. Adams 178. Evans 14145.

A Congregational clergyman and president of Harvard, Langdon had a reputation as a 'zealous Whig' and patriot. This sermon reinforces that reputation, for his descriptions of the Battle of Lexington are somewhat prejudiced. For example, he describes the British Regulars as making a practice of 'snatching morsels of bread' from the mouths of weeping children.

On the eve of the Revolution most leaders of the American opposition to Britain defended the status quo and supported traditional constitutional principles. These ideologues, almost to a man, were country gentlemen, lawyers, ministers, or merchants, precisely the ones with the most to lose should the socioeconomic situation change as a result of British interference. Ac- cordingly, when they became convinced that the corrupt forces which prevailed in England were about to dominate America, and that America's destiny was in serious jeopardy, they felt obligated to preserve the 'virtuous Principles' of their ancestors and themselves, and they opted for independence.

121 THOMAS JEFFERSON (1743–1826)

A Summary View of the Rights of British America

Philadelphia, 1774. Adams 119b. Evans 13351. Gift of Frederick Lewis Gay, 1918.

Identified from the outset with the aggressive anti-British group in Virginia, Jefferson was one of the authors of the resolves creating the Virginia Committee of Correspondence. Prevented by illness from attending the Virginia convention of 1774, for which he had drawn up the resolutions of his county and been appointed a delegate, he sent this *Summary View*, which proved to be the greatest literary contribution to the American Revolution next to the Declaration of Independence. He emphasized the 'natural' right of emigration and the right of conquest exercised by the first English settlers in America. He denied all parliamentary authority over the colonies, and claimed only voluntary loyalty to the king. This and his other writings during the period stressed 'rights as derived from nature,' not a king. Here, as elsewhere, he strove for the 'revindication of Saxon liberties' and the renewal of original principles.

122 JAMES WILSON (1742–1798)

Considerations on the Nature and the Extent of the Legislative Authority of the British Parliament

Philadelphia, 1774. Adams 149. Evans 13775.

Born in Scotland, Wilson emigrated to Pennsylvania in 1765 in the midst of the Stamp Act disturbances. He became the head of a committee of correspondence at Carlisle, Pennsylvania, and was a delegate to the First Continental Congress in 1774. Upon arriving at the Congress he distributed this pamphlet, which concluded that Parliament had no authority over the colonies in any instance. Only a few had taken such an advanced position even by 1774, but Wilson had come to this conclusion four years before he published this essay.

123 ALEXANDER HAMILTON (1757–1804)

A Full Vindication of the Measures of the Congress, From the Calumnies of their Enemies; In Answer to . . . A. W. Farmer

New York, 1774. Adams 116. Evans 13313. Gift of Alfred L. Aiken, 1941.

Hamilton wrote this tract while a seventeen-year-old student at Kings College (later Columbia) in New York. He spoke against British measures in July 1774 and began writing for *The New York Journal, or General Advertiser* with a vigor which attracted attention. In December he wrote this pamphlet, and when Samuel Seabury replied, he continued the debate in *The Farmer Refuted*. Hamilton's position was that of a moderate who loyally defended the king's sovereignty but rejected the pretensions of Parliament.

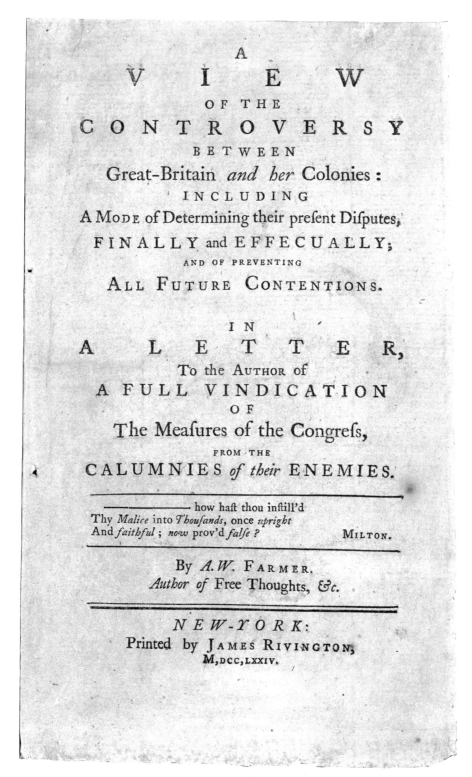

A

V I E W

OF THE

C O N T R O V E R S Y

BETWEEN

Great-Britain *and her* Colonies:

INCLUDING

A MODE of Determining their prefent Difputes,

FINALLY and EFFECUALLY;

AND OF PREVENTING

ALL FUTURE CONTENTIONS.

IN

A L E T T E R,

To the AUTHOR of

A FULL VINDICATION

OF

The Meafures of the Congrefs,

FROM THE

CALUMNIES *of their* ENEMIES.

——————— how haft thou inftill'd
Thy *Malice* into *Thoufands*, once *upright*
And *faithful* ; *now* prov'd *falfe* ?   MILTON.

By *A.W.* FARMER.
Author of Free Thoughts, *&c.*

N E W - Y O R K :
Printed by JAMES RIVINGTON,
M,DCC,LXXIV.

124. One of Samuel Seabury's loyalist pamphlets

124 SAMUEL SEABURY (1729–1796)

A View of the Controversy Between Great-Britain and her Colonies

New York, 1774. Adams 137a. Evans 13603. Gift of Alfred L. Aiken, 1941.

This Tory tract was written by Samuel Seabury, who became the first bishop of the Episcopal Church in America. During the imperial crisis, Seabury undertook a major literary struggle to keep the colonies loyal to the crown. His most important pamphlets, like this one, were signed 'A. W. Farmer.' With clear and forceful language he attempted to convince Americans that their freedom and greatest good lay in remaining loyal to the British government and in securing the changes they desired through peaceful and orderly appeals. These pamphlets were ably answered by seventeen-year-old Alexander Hamilton, a student in Kings College.

125 DANIEL LEONARD (1740–1829)

'Massachusettensis'

[Boston, 1775.] Adams 180b. Evans 14157.

Leonard was a lawyer and determined loyalist who was a member of the provincial aristocracy in Massachusetts. In 1774 he began writing a series of seventeen articles in defense of crown policies, first published in the *Massachusetts Gazette* (1774–1775) over the signature 'Massachusettensis.' John Adams replied to these over the signature 'Novanglus.'

126 JOHN ADAMS (1735–1826)

'Novanglus'

Boston Gazette and Country Journal, January 23, 1775.

Adams, an active patriot during the controversy with England, composed these essays in response to articles written by Daniel Leonard under the pseudonym 'Massachusettensis' in the Tory newspaper the *Massachusetts Gazette.* Leonard had argued that only by remaining loyal and subservient to Parliament and the crown could the colonies remain free. Adams countered by pointing out that Parliament had been the source of most of the economic problems afflicting the colonies, and that only by asserting their constitutional rights could the colonists remain free.

127 JOHN ADAMS (1735–1826)

Thoughts on Government: Applicable to the Present State of the American Colonies

Philadelphia, 1776. Adams 205a. Evans 14639.

Adams, who became the second president of the United States, was a member of the Continental Congress when he wrote this pamphlet. In it, he asserted that 'the form of government, which communicates ease, comfort, security, or in one word happiness to the greatest degree is the best.' He added that 'there is no good government but what is Republican,' and that the best part of the British constitution was the adherence to the principles that 'an Empire of Laws, and not of Men,' constituted the best government. Adams concluded that he and his fellow Americans lived at a time 'when the greatest lawgivers of antiquity would have wished to have lived,' for there had never been a time in history when 'three millions of people [had] full power and a fair opportunity to form and establish the wisest and happiest government that human wisdom can contrive.'

Tensions between Great Britain and her colonies eased from late 1770 through 1772. Early in 1773, when the committees of correspondence were formed, relations again became strained and radical leaders became dominant in the New England and southern colonies. The Tea Act and the Intolerable Acts led to critical confrontations. The situation in America became explosive.

Late in 1774, the First Continental Congress convened in Philadelphia and deliberated the future of the American colonies. Moderates prevailed even though armed conflict broke out in April 1775. The balance was finally tipped in favor of independence by the king's Proclamation of Rebellion, by Thomas Paine's pamphlet *Common Sense*, and by the activities of radical politicians. When the Continental Congress declared independence in July 1776, however, it insisted that the new nation was the conservative defender of law and liberty, and that the British were the ones guilty of subverting the constitution and making radical innovations.

128

Boston, April 9, 1773, Sir, The Committee of Correspondence of this Town . . .

[Boston, 1773.] Evans 12689.

Indicative of the growing unity of interest among the colonists against the policies of Great Britain is this broadside letter received by Boston's Committee of Correspondence. The Virginia House of Burgesses sent the letter to inform Boston of the creation of a standing committee of correspondence and to assure the New Englanders of Virginia's continued support in the constitutional crisis. The letter also asked that other committees of correspondence be maintained in the assemblies of the other colonies. This prelude to the First Continental Congress expanded the committees of correspondence in the colonies.

129

Boston, December, 1773

[Boston], 1773. Evans 12694.

This broadside describes a meeting of the people of Boston on November 29 and 30, 1773, to determine the most effective way to prevent the 'unloading, receiving or vending the detestable Tea sent out by the East-India Company.' Two weeks later the problem was resolved with the Boston Tea Party.

130   JOHN JOHNSTON (1753–1818)

Green Dragon Tavern

Pen and ink drawing with watercolor wash, 1773.

Taverns and church meeting halls were traditional gathering places in the colonies. The Green Dragon Tavern, in the North End of Boston, was the meeting place for the local Sons of Liberty, a self-appointed association of colonists dedicated to fighting the Stamp Act and subsequent legislation. It was here, according to the inscription on this contemporary sketch, that the Boston Tea Party was planned in December 1773. Few watercolor views of eighteenth-century Boston survive.

131

Tea Leaves from the Boston Tea Party

Gift of Thaddeus M. Harris, 1840.

This bottle contains some of the tea that was thrown into Boston Harbor on December 16, 1773. The tea was given to the American Antiquarian Society by the

130. The Boston Tea Party was planned at the Green Dragon Tavern

Rev. Thaddeus M. Harris (1768–1842) who was five years old when he gathered up the tea on the beaches of Dorchester Neck where it had been carried by the tide.

132 JOLLEY ALLEN (1716–1782?)

'An Account of Part of the Suffering and Losses of Mr. Jolley Allen a Native of London.'

Minute Book, Manuscript.

This autobiography describes the life of Jolley Allen, who came to Boston with his family in 1755 and became a successful merchant. During the years of crisis after 1763 he sided with the British. As a loyalist he suffered at the hands of the patriots and lost almost everything he had. The opening pages of the account tell of Allen's ordeal in 1772–1773 because of his compliance with the Tea Act and his purchase of two chests of tea from Governor Hutchinson's sons. Loyalists were not treated kindly during this period and Allen's experiences were not atypical.

133 JOHN CORNISH (active 1751–1825)

Portrait of Charles Paxton (1708–1788)

Oil painting, ca. 1751. Gift of 'A Lady,' 1814.

For several years before the Revolution and during the tea crisis, Paxton served as one of the British commissioners of customs at Boston. After seizing one of John Hancock's vessels for smuggling, Paxton was hanged in effigy from the 'Liberty Tree.' As a result, he encouraged Governor Hutchinson to send for the first troops to come to Boston. A loyalist, he fled Boston in 1776 with the British army and eventually settled in London. He longed to return to America but his property had been confiscated and he had been banished.

This portrait was painted in England well before the Revolution.

134

From the Pennsylvania Packet. Philadelphia, October 3

[Philadelphia, 1774.] Bristol 3803. MP 42604.

The theme of a corrupt England conspiring against American liberty was expressed in this broadside. The author lamented the British conduct toward the Americans and declared that any man 'made up of American Flesh and Blood' must defend himself and his country from the scathing comments levelled by the British. Although the writer considered himself a moderate man, his experiences in England had convinced him that 'Firmness on the Part of the Americans will insure them the Victory.' He added that the people of England 'are sunk in Luxury, and wish only to get their Hands into the Purse of the Americans to support them in it.' He concluded by urging the colonists to 'struggle like Men for your dear Inheritance.'

135

Liberty Triumphant: or the Downfall of Oppression

Engraving, Philadelphia, 1774.

This political cartoon (which has been attributed to Henry Dawkins) deals with the tea crisis late in 1773 and early in 1774. As is typical of eighteenth-century political prints, the meaning is not easy to decipher, but the numbered figures are identified below the print. Lord North (1) and Lord Bute (2) are easily recognized. Dr. John Kearsley, Jr., of Philadelphia, an outspoken loyalist, is represented by figure 4. Figure 6 refers to the authors of Tory articles in the *New York Gazetteer*. Figures 7 through 9 refer to the East India Company, and numbers 10 and 11 are allegorical allusions to corruption in England. Figures 12 through 18 represent the American side. The cartoon reviews the situation from the Whig point of view, and its meaning would have been familiar to anyone living in Philadelphia or New York.

From the Pennsylvania Packet.

PHILADELPHIA, *October* 3.

Extract of a Letter from a Gentleman in Bristol, to his Friend in this City, dated July 20, 1774.

" SURROUNDED as I am by a thousand various Businesses, still I cannot resist the strong Inclination I feel to tell you that I am alive and well once more in old England; formerly I loved the Country and People, but now both appear odious to me; their Conduct towards the Americans is horrid, cruel and detestable; they call ye all Thieves, Pirates, and Rebels, for which in Return, I make no Scruple to call them Knaves, Scoundrels, and spiritless *Slaves*. Every Day I am in the most furious Quarrels in Vindication of America, that ever you saw--- I wish to God that you had a few more Friends in this City---I shall, through my zealous Attachment lose or endanger my Election; but no Matter; they already cry, *no American*---no Bill of Rights Man. My Acquaintance tell me I am too warm; but do you tell me, my Friend, who that is made up of American Flesh and Blood can sit calm and composed to hear his native Country, with his dearest Connections calumniated, belied and reprobated. No, by Heaven and Earth, I swear! I never will silently put up with such Ill-usage while I have Breath to speak, or Hands to fight.

" I am just returned from London: It is with a Degree of Pleasure, I can assure you, many of the great Men are ashamed of what they have done, seriously dreading the Associations and Resentment of the Virginians in particular: The Revenue arising from the Duties on Tobacco is *mortgaged*, and *a Stop to their Exportations* would make a glorious Confusion among their High Mightinesses.

" When I left America, I recommended Moderation; but with Concern I find, *that* Conduct will not do---Resentment must shew itself, for our Ministers wish themselves well out of it. *Firmness* on the Part of the Americans will insure them the Victory, now is the Crisis, the important Crisis, of your whole Lives---you can *lose nothing* by a patriotic Stand---you may *gain every Thing*.

" The People of this Country are sunk in Luxury, and wish only to get their Hands into the Purse of the Americans to support them in it---They are totally indifferent about Liberty, and lost to every Sense of Honour or Virtue; open Corruption is connived at and approved; Oppression, black as Hell, darkens the Annals of the present Times; and Britons seem happy in their supine Folly and *base Vassalage*.

" If once the Americans submit, I foresee a Train of Evils ready to light upon them: Taxes, Impositions and Oppressions, without Moderation or End. Now is the appointed Time to struggle like Men for your dear Inheritance; and there can be no Doubt but Providence, and a *new Parliament*, will do you ample Justice. I will weary Heaven with my Prayers for your Success.---My sincere good Wishes attend you, and all the rest of my worthy Countrymen in Philadelphia."

134. A letter from an American in England supporting resistance

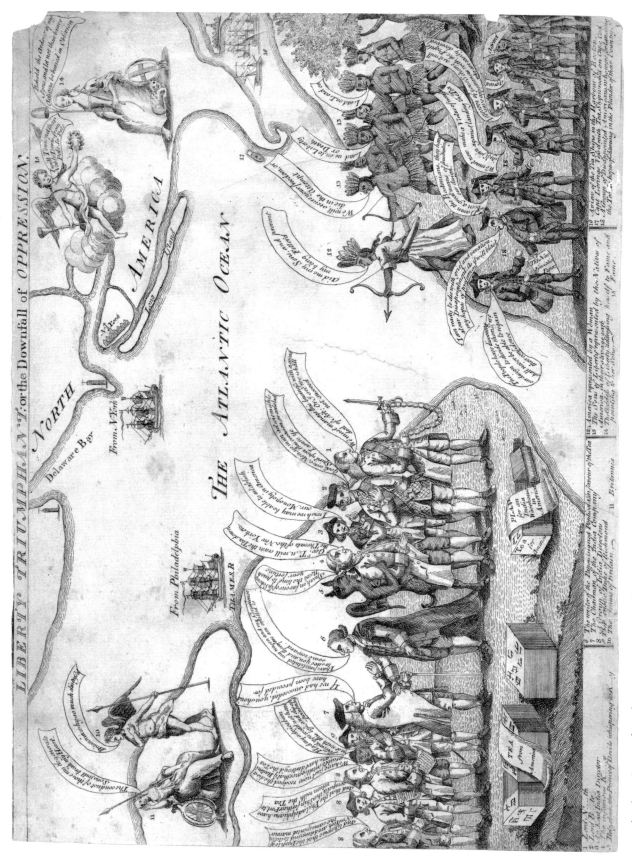

135. An American political cartoon satirizing the tea crisis

136

A New Method of Macarony Making, as Practised at Boston in North America

Mezzotint, London, [1774]. British Museum Catalogue 5232.

This is a satire on the treatment given to John Malcomb, the unpopular commissioner of customs, at Boston. On January 27, 1774, Malcomb had been tarred and feathered, led to the gallows with a rope round his neck, and forced to drink enormous quantities of tea. His offense was attempting to collect customs duties. The incident was not connected to the Boston Tea Party; rather it was indicative of the constant tension between the British and colonists.

The title is ironical, for 'Macarony' in the eighteenth century referred to dandies and fops who dressed in an exaggerated manner. The Bostonian with the cockade on his hat is one of the Sons of Liberty, and the number 45 on the other American's hat is a reference to John Wilkes's *North Briton*, Number 45.

137

The Boston Port Act in a Serious Address to the Inhabitants of the Colony of New-York

New York, 1774. Adams 138. Evans 13605.

This act along with the Justice Act and the Massachusetts Government Act were known collectively as the Coercive Acts. These measures closed the port of Boston, forcing the removal of the colonial capital to Salem, restricted town meetings, and deprived the Massachusetts House of Representatives of several of its long-cherished powers. These acts persuaded many hesitant colonists to side with the patriots. This pamphlet in particular urged the other colonies to aid Boston.

138 PAUL REVERE (1735–1818)

The Able Doctor, or America Swallowing the Bitter Draught

Engraving, [Boston], *The Royal American Magazine*, [June 1774]. Stauffer 2673.

'The Able Doctor,' copied by Revere from a print in the *London Magazine* for April 1774, depicts Lord North forcing tea down the throat of America, represented as an Indian princess. Britannia hides her head in shame. Reference is made here to the Boston Tea Party and the Boston Port Bill which closed the port to all traffic. In this issue of *The Royal American Magazine* is an 'Historical Chronicle' for June describing the political and economic conditions in Boston as a result of the Port Bill which went into effect on June 1, 1774. Paul Revere, engraver and silversmith, was a member of the Sons of Liberty. He worked closely with the leading patriots to provide graphic depictions for some of their polemics.

139 PAUL REVERE (1735–1818)

The Mitred Minuet

Engraving, [Boston], *The Royal American Magazine*, [October 1774]. Stauffer 2688.

Revere's engraving of 'The Mitred Minuet' was copied from a plate in the *London Magazine* for July 1774. Four bishops dance around the Quebec Act as Lord Bute, Lord North, the devil, and another minister look on. The Quebec Act provided religious freedom for the French Catholics in Canada in exchange for their loyalty to the crown. New Englanders classed the Quebec Act with the Boston Port Act, the Massachusetts Government Act, the Administration of Justice Act, and the Quartering Act as the five Intolerable Acts. The text which accompanies the engraving describes the print in terms of a vision. The narrator is puzzled over the sanction given to Catholicism. Although the *London Magazine* was imported into the colonies, the inclusion of this cartoon and others in *The Royal American Magazine* guaranteed an even wider circulation in America.

140

We the Subscribers of the [District] of [Charlton]

[Boston, 1774.] Evans 13163.

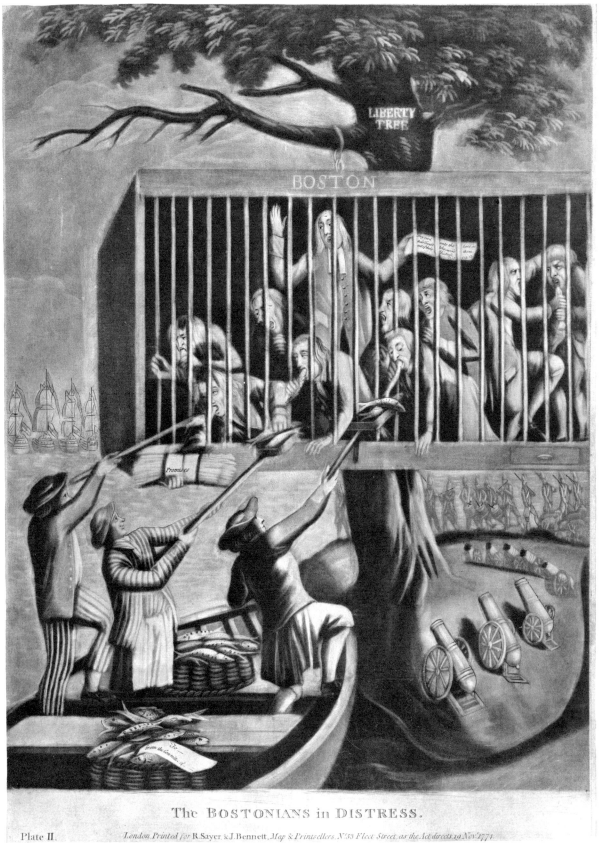

The BOSTONIANS in DISTRESS.

Plate II.   London. Printed for R.Sayer & J.Bennett, Map & Printsellers. N.º 53 Fleet Street, as the Act directs 19 Nov. 1774.

141. An English satire on the punishment meted out to Boston for the Tea Party

A DECLARATION

By the Representatives of the

United Colonies

Of NORTH-AMERICA, now met in

General Congress

At PHILADELPHIA,

Setting forth the CAUSES and NECESSITY

Of their taking up

ARMS.

A View of that great and flourishing City or BOSTON, when in its purity, and out of the Hands of the Philistines.

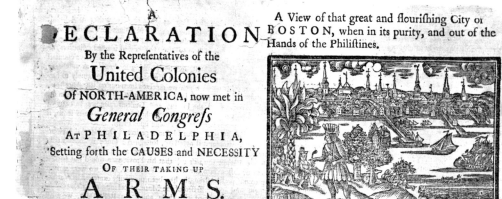

IF it was possible for Men, who exercise their Reason, to believe, that the Divine Author of our Existence intended a Part of the human Race to hold an absolute Property in, and an unbounded Power over others, marked out by his Infinite Goodness & Wisdom, as the Objects of a legal Domination, never rightfully resistible, however severe and oppressive, the Inhabitants of these Colonies might at least require from the Parliament of Great Britain, some Evidence, that this dreadful Authority over them has been granted to that Body. But a Reverence for our Great CREATOR, Principles of Humanity, and the Dictates of common Sense, must convince all those who reflect upon the Subject, that Government was instituted to promote the Welfare of Mankind, and ought to be administered for the Attainment of that End. The Legislature of Great-Britain, however stimulated by an inordinate Passion for a Power not only unjustifiable, but which they know to be peculiarly reprobated by the very Constitution of that Kingdom, and desperate of Success in any Mode of Contest, where Regard should be had to Truth, Law, or Right, have at length, deserting those, attempted to effect their cruel and impolitic Purpose of enslaving these Colonies by Violence, and have thereby rendered it necessary for us to close with their last Appeal from Reason to Arms.—Yet however blinded that Assembly may be, by their intemperate Rage for unlimited Domination so to slight Justice and the Opinion of Mankind, we esteem ourselves bound by Obligations of Respect to the rest of the World, to make known the Justice of our Cause.

Our Forefathers, Inhabitants of the Island of Great-Britain, left their native Land to seek on these Shores a Residence for civil and religious Freedom. At the Expence of their Blood, at the Hazard of their Fortunes, without the least Charge to the Country from which they removed, by unceasing Labor and an unconquerable Spirit, they effected Settlements in the distant & inhospitable Wilds of America, then filled with numerous and warlike Nations of Barbarians.—Societies or Governments, vested with perfect Legislatures, were formed under Charters from the Crown, and an harmonious Intercourse was established between the Colonies and the Kingdom from which they derived their Origin.—The mutual Benefits of this Union became in a short Time so extraordinary, as to excite Astonishment: It is universally confessed, that the amazing Increase of the Wealth, Strength and Navigation of the Realm, arose from this Source; and the Minister who so wisely and successfully directed the Measures of Great-Britain in the late War, publicly declared, that these Colonies enabled her to triumph over her Enemies.—Towards the Conclusion of that War, it pleased our Sovereign to make a Change in his Counsels.—From that fatal Moment, the Affairs of the British Empire began to fall into Confusion, and gradually sliding from the Summit of glorious Prosperity to which they had been advanced by the Virtues and Abilities of one Man, are at length distated by the Convulsions that now shake it to its deepest Foundations.— The new Ministry finding the brave Foes of Britain, though frequently defeated, yet still contending, took up the unfortunate Idea of granting them a hasty Peace, and of then subduing her faithful Friends.

These devoted Colonies were judged to be in such a State, as to present Victories without Bloodshed, and all the easy Emoluments of statuteable Plunder.— The uninterrupted Tenor of their peaceable and respectful Behaviour from the Beginning of Colonization, their dutiful, zealous and useful Services during the War, though so recently and amply acknowledged in the most honorable Manner by his Majesty, by the late King, and by Parliament, could not save them from the meditated Innovations.— Parliament was influenced to adopt the pernicious Project, & assuming a new Power over them, have in the Course of eleven Years, given such decisive Specimens of the Spirit and Consequences attending this Power, as to leave no Doubt concerning the Effects of Acquiescence under it. They have undertaken to give and grant our Money without our Consent, tho'

we have ever exercised an exclusive Right to dispose of our own Property; Statutes have been passed for extending the Jurisdiction of Courts of Admiralty and Vice Admiralty beyond their ancient Limits: For depriving us of the accustomed and inestimable Privilege of Trial by Jury in Cases affecting both Life and Property; for suspending the Legislature of one of the Colonies; for interdicting all Commerce of another; and for altering fundamentally the Form of Government established by Charter, and secured by Acts of its own Legislature solemnly confirmed by the Crown; for exempting the "Murderers" of Colonists from legal Trial, and in Effect, from Punishment; for erecting in a neighbouring Province acquired by the joint Arms of Great Britain and America, a Despotism dangerous to our very Existence; and for quartering Soldiers upon the Colonists in Time of profound Peace. It has also been resolved in Parliament, that Colonists charged with committing certain Offences, shall be transported to England to be tried.

But why should we enumerate our Injuries in Detail? By one Statute it is declared, that Parliament can " of Right make Laws to bind us IN ALL CASES WHATSOEVER." What is to defend us against so enormous, so unlimited a Power? Not a single Man of those who assume it, is chosen by us; or is subject to our Controul or Influence: but on the contrary, they are all of them exempt from the Operation of such Laws, and an American Revenue, if not diverted from the ostensible Purposes for which it is raised, would actually lighten their own Burdens in Proportion, as they increase ours. We saw the Misery to which such Despotism would reduce us. We for ten Years incessantly and ineffectually besieged the Throne as Supplicants; we reasoned, we remonstrated with Parliament in the most mild and decent Language. But Administration, sensible that we should regard those oppressive Measures as Freemen ought to do, sent over Fleets and Armies to enforce them. The Indignation of the Americans was roused it is true; but it was the Indignation of a virtuous, loyal, and affectionate People. A Congress of Delegates from the united Colonies was assembled at Philadelphia, on the fifth Day of last September. We resolved again to offer an humble and dutiful Petition to the King, and also addressed our Fellow Subjects of Great Britain. We have pursued every temperate, every respectful Measure, we have even proceeded to break off our commercial Intercourse with our Fellow Subjects, as the last peaceable Admonition, that our Attachment to no Nation upon Earth should supplant our Attachment to Liberty.— This, we flattered ourselves, was the ultimate Step of the Controversy: But subsequent Events have shewn, how vain was this Hope of finding Moderation in our Enemies.

Several threatening Expressions against the Colonies were inserted in his Majesty's Speech; our Petition, though we were told it was a decent one, that his Majesty had been pleased to receive it graciously, and to promise laying it before his Parliament, was huddled into both Houses amongst a Bundle of American Papers, and there neglected. The Lords and Commons in their Address, in the Month of February last, said, "that a Rebellion at that Time actually existed within the Province of Massachusetts Bay; and that those concerned in it, had been countenanced and encouraged by unlawful Combinations and Engagements, entered into by his Majesty's Subjects in several of the other Colonies; and therefore they besought his Majesty, " that he would take the most effectual Measures to inforce due Obedience to the Laws and Authority of the supreme Legislature."— Soon after the commercial Intercourse of whole Colonies, with foreign Countries and with each other, was cut off by an Act of Parliament; by another, several of them were intirely prohibited from the Fisheries in the Seas near their Coasts, on which they always depended for their Sustenance; and large Reinforcements of Ships and Troops were immediately sent over to General Gage.

Fruitless were all the Entreaties, Arguments and Eloquence of an

144. A declaration by the Continental Congress in 1775 on the reasons for taking up arms

This is a protest against the Boston Port Bill as circulated in the town of Charlton in June 1774. Those who signed this petition agreed to suspend all trade with England, to no longer purchase or consume English goods, and to boycott merchants who refused to sign the petition. Similar compacts were circulated throughout Massachusetts.

141

The Bostonians in Distress

Mezzotint, London, 1774. British Museum Catalogue 5241.

In this political cartoon a cage inscribed 'Boston' hangs from a branch of the 'Liberty Tree.' In it are ten hungry Bostonians being fed fish by three men. This and other symbolic representations refer to the closing of the port of Boston. Many people suffered as a result. Gifts of food and other items were sent from all the other colonies to ease the Bostonians' distress. The artist's irony seems directed against both sides, for the English soldiers direct their cannon at the 'Liberty Tree' while the cage, symbol of slavery and barbarity, hangs on the 'Liberty Tree.'

142

Proceedings of the Grand American Continental Congress at Philadelphia, September 5, 1774

Portsmouth, New Hampshire, [1774]. Bristol 3891. MP 42735.

By early August 1774 it had been agreed that a congress would meet in Philadelphia in September. Every colony but Georgia chose delegates, either officially through colonial assemblies or extralegally through 'provincial congresses,' which in most places were rump sessions of prorogued assemblies. This broadside contains the proceedings of Congress for its first session. After listing the actions taken by Parliament and the ministry to 'enslave' America, a new non-importation agreement is called for to last until the hated parliamentary measures were revoked. This

broadside was printed as an extra of the *New Hampshire Gazette*.

143

The Poor Man's Advice to his Poor Neighbours: A Ballad

New York, 1774. Evans 13551. Gift of C. Waller Barrett, 1956.

This anonymous Tory ballad satirized the Continental Congress and the American rebels. It praised King George, and treated the patriots as ignorant children who did not know how well off they were. The ballad also protested congressional control over what the colonists could eat, read, buy, and sell. It closed with an ironical blast at the tyranny of Congress.

144

A Declaration by the Representatives of the United Colonies of North-America, Now Met in General Congress at Philadelphia, Setting forth the Causes and Necessity Of Their Taking Up Arms

Portsmouth, New Hampshire, 1775. Evans 14550.

This declaration by the Continental Congress bemoaning the state of affairs in Boston harkened back to a purer, simpler time. After listing the 'evils' inflicted upon America by 'corrupt ministries' over the past decade, the congress asserted that it was the duty of everyone to defend the 'Freedom that is our Birthright' and take up arms against the aggressor.

The cut is of Boston when it was 'in its purity, and out of the Hands of the Philistines.' Engraved by James Turner in the 1740s, it depicts an idyllic city.

145

To the Inhabitants of the City and County of New-York

[New York, 1775.] Evans 14505. Gift of Thomas W. Streeter, 1967.

This broadside attacks merchants in New York who had been supplying Gage's troops in Boston with necessities 'for effecting the immediate destruction of our brethren and fellow-subjects in Boston.' A small committee of merchants and others had been unable to stop such practices so a mass meeting was called at the 'Liberty-pole' to determine how best to deal with the offenders. The meeting took place on April 15, 1775. The general tenor of the crowd left little doubt among loyalists that New Yorkers were primed for battle.

146 THOMAS PAINE (1737–1809)

Common Sense

Philadelphia, 1776. Adams 222a. Evans 14954. Gift of Richard Gimbel, 1955.

Paine was an English-born, revolutionary political pamphleteer and agitator. *Common Sense* was published anonymously in Philadelphia on January 10, 1776, and sold for two shillings. It urged an immediate declaration of independence as the fulfillment of America's moral obligation to the world. The colonies must fall away eventually, Paine said; a continent could not remain tied to an island. If these colonies could manage to free themselves from a vicious monarchy, while their society was still uncorrupt, they could alter human destiny by their example.

147

Portrait of Thomas Paine (1737–1809)

Oil painting. Gift of R. Henniker-Heaton (1930).

This portrait of Thomas Paine was painted in the first quarter of the nineteenth century and has been attributed to several artists, including Rembrandt Peale, the son of Charles Willson Peale. The globe at Paine's elbow is labelled 'American Independence' and Paine holds a copy of his influential *Common Sense*.

148

In Congress, July 4, 1776. A Declaration by the Representatives of the United States of America, In General Congress Assembled

Salem, 1776. Evans 15163.

This broadside edition of America's most famous document was ordered printed by the Revolutionary Council of the State of Massachusetts. A copy was to be sent to the 'Ministers of each Parish of every Denomination, within this State,' so that it could be read to their respective congregations. The ministers were to deliver their copies to the 'Clerks of their several Towns or Districts,' who were required to record the Declaration in their 'respective Town, or District Books, there to remain as a perpetual Memorial therof.'

The Declaration of Independence was revolutionary in two ways. First, it put the formal stamp of approval on colonial resistance to the British. Secondly, it signalled not only American rejection of Britain but American faith in the New World. Monarchy and hereditary aristocracy were permanently removed. The decks were therefore cleared for American republicanism, a novel experiment whose outcome could not be predicted, even by its most ardent supporters. Independence, therefore, was both a rejection of the past and a 'leap into the dark.' It was a terrible risk.

IN CONGRESS,
JULY 4, 1776.

A DECLARATION
BY THE
REPRESENTATIVES
OF THE
UNITED STATES OF AMERICA,
IN GENERAL CONGRESS ASSEMBLED.

WHEN in the Course of human Events, it becomes necessary for one People to dissolve the political Bands which have connected them with another, and to assume among the Powers of the Earth, the separate and equal Station to which the Laws of Nature and of Nature's God entitle them, a decent Respect to the Opinions of Mankind requires that they should declare the Causes which impel them to the Separation.

We hold these Truths to be self-evident, that all Men are created equal, that they are endowed by their Creator with certain unalienable Rights, that among these are Life, Liberty, and the Pursuit of Happiness :—That to secure these Rights, Governments are instituted among Men, deriving their just Powers from the Consent of the Governed, that whenever any Form of Government becomes destructive of these Ends, it is the Right of the People to alter or to abolish it, and to institute a new Government, laying its Foundation on such Principles, and organizing its Powers in such Form, as to them shall seem most likely to effect their Safety and Happiness. Prudence, indeed, will dictate that Governments long established should not be changed for light and transient Causes ; and accordingly all Experience hath shewn, that Mankind are more disposed to suffer, while Evils are sufferable, than to right themselves by abolishing the Forms to which they are accustomed. But when a long Train of Abuses and Usurpations, pursuing invariably the same Object, evinces a Design to reduce them under absolute Despotism, it is their Right, it is their Duty, to throw off such Government, and to provide new Guards for their future Security. Such has been the patient Sufferance of these Colonies ; and such is now the Necessity which constrains them to alter their former Systems of Government. The History of the present King of Great-Britain is a History of repeated Injuries and Usurpations, all having in direct Object the Establishment of an absolute Tyranny over these States. To prove this, let Facts be submitted to a candid World.

He has refused his Assent to Laws, the most wholesome and necessary for the public Good.

He has forbidden his Governors to pass Laws of immediate and pressing Importance, unless suspended in their Operation until his Assent should be obtained ; and when so suspended, he has utterly neglected to attend to them.

He has refused to pass other Laws for the Accommodation of large Districts of People, unless those People would relinquish the Right of Representation in the Legislature, a Right inestimable to them, and formidable to Tyrants only.

He has called together Legislative Bodies at Places unusual, uncomfortable, and distant from the Depository of their public Records, for the sole Purpose of fatiguing them into Compliance with his Measures.

He has dissolved Representative Houses repeatedly, for opposing with manly Firmness his Invasions on the Rights of the People.

He has refused for a long Time, after such Dissolutions, to cause others to be elected ; whereby the Legislative Powers, incapable of Annihilation, have returned to the People at large for their Exercise ; the State remaining in the mean Time exposed to all the Dangers of Invasion from without, and Convulsions within.

He has endeavoured to prevent the Population of these States ; for that Purpose obstructing the Laws for Naturalization of Foreigners ; refusing to pass others to encourage their Migrations hither, and raising the Conditions of new Appropriations of Lands.

He has obstructed the Administration of Justice, by refusing his Assent to Laws for establishing Judiciary Powers.

He has made Judges dependent on his Will alone, for the Tenure of their Offices, and the Amount and Payment of their Salaries.

He has erected a multitude of new Offices, and sent hither Swarms of Officers to harrass our People, and eat out their Substance.

He has kept among us, in Times of Peace, Standing Armies, without the Consent of our Legislatures.

He has affected to render the Military independent of, and superior to the Civil Power.

He has combined with others to subject us to a Jurisdiction foreign to our Constitution, and unacknowledged by our Laws ; giving his Assent to their Acts of pretended Legislation :

For quartering large Bodies of armed Troops among us :

For protecting them, by a mock Trial, from Punishment for any Murders which they should commit on the Inhabitants of these States :

For cutting off our Trade with all Parts of the World :

For imposing Taxes on us without our Consent :

For depriving us, in many Cases, of the Benefits of Trial by Jury :

For transporting us beyond Seas to be tried for pretended Offences :

For abolishing the free System of English Laws in a neighbouring Province, establishing therein an arbitrary Government, and enlarging its Boundaries, so as to render it at once an Example and fit Instrument for introducing the same absolute Rule into these Colonies :

For taking away our Charters, abolishing our most valuable Laws, and altering fundamentally the Forms of our Governments :

For suspending our own Legislatures, and declaring themselves invested with Power to legislate for us in all Cases whatsoever.

He has abdicated Government here, by declaring us out of his Protection and waging War against us.

He has plundered our Seas, ravaged our Coasts, burnt our Towns, and destroyed the Lives of our People.

He is, at this Time, transporting large Armies of foreign Mercenaries to compleat the Works of Death, Desolation, and Tyranny, already begun with Circumstances of Cruelty and Perfidy scarcely paralleled in the most barbarous Ages, and totally unworthy the Head of a civilized Nation.

He has constrained our Fellow Citizens, taken Captive on the high Seas, to bear Arms against their Country, to become the Executioners of their Friends and Brethren, or to fall themselves by their Hands.

He has excited Domestic Insurrections amongst us, and has endeavoured to bring on the Inhabitants of our Frontiers, the merciless Indian Savages, whose known Rule of Warfare, is an undistinguished Destruction of all Ages, Sexes, and Conditions.

In every Stage of these Oppressions we have petitioned for Redress, in the most humble Terms : Our repeated Petitions have been answered only by repeated Injury !—A Prince, whose Character is thus marked by every Act which may define a Tyrant, is unfit to be the Ruler of a Free People !

Nor have we been wanting in Attention to our British Brethren. We have warned them from Time to Time of Attempts by their Legislature to extend an unwarrantable Jurisdiction over us. We have reminded them of the Circumstances of our Emigration and Settlement here. We have appealed to their native Justice and Magnanimity, and we have conjured them by the Ties of our common Kindred to disavow these Usurpations, which would inevitably interrupt our Connexions and Correspondence. They too have been deaf to the Voice of Justice and of Consanguinity. We must, therefore, acquiesce in the Necessity which denounces our Separation, and hold them, as we hold the rest of Mankind, Enemies in War ; in Peace, Friends.

We, therefore, the Representatives of the United States of America, in General Congress assembled, appealing to the Supreme Judge of the World for the Rectitude of our Intentions, do, in the Name and by the Authority of the good People of these Colonies, solemnly Publish and Declare, That these United Colonies are, and of Right ought to be, Free and Independent States ; that they are absolved from all Allegiance to the British Crown ; and that all political Connexion between them and the State of Great-Britain, is, and ought to be totally dissolved ; and that as Free and Independent States, they have full Power to levy War, conclude Peace, contract Alliances, establish Commerce, and to do all other Acts and Things which Independent States may of Right do. And for the Support of this Declaration, with a firm Reliance on the Protection of Divine Providence, we mutually pledge to each other our Lives, our Fortunes, and our Sacred Honor.

Signed by Order *and in* Behalf *of the* Congress,
JOHN HANCOCK, President.
Attest, CHARLES THOMPSON, Secretary.

IN COUNCIL, July 17th, 1776.

ORDERED, That the Declaration of Independence be printed ; and a Copy sent to the Ministers of each Parish, of every Denomination, within this State ; and that they severally be required to read the same to their respective Congregations, as soon as divine Service is ended, in the Afternoon, on the first Lord's-Day after they shall have received it :---And after such Publication thereof, to deliver the said Declaration to the Clerks of their several Towns, or Districts ; who are hereby required to record the same in their respective Town, or District Books, there to remain as a perpetual Memorial thereof.

In the Name, and by Order of the Council, R. DERBY, Jun. President.

A true Copy Attest, John Avery, Dep. Sec'y.

SALEM, Massachusetts-Bay : Printed by E. Russell, by Order of Authority.

148. The Declaration of Independence

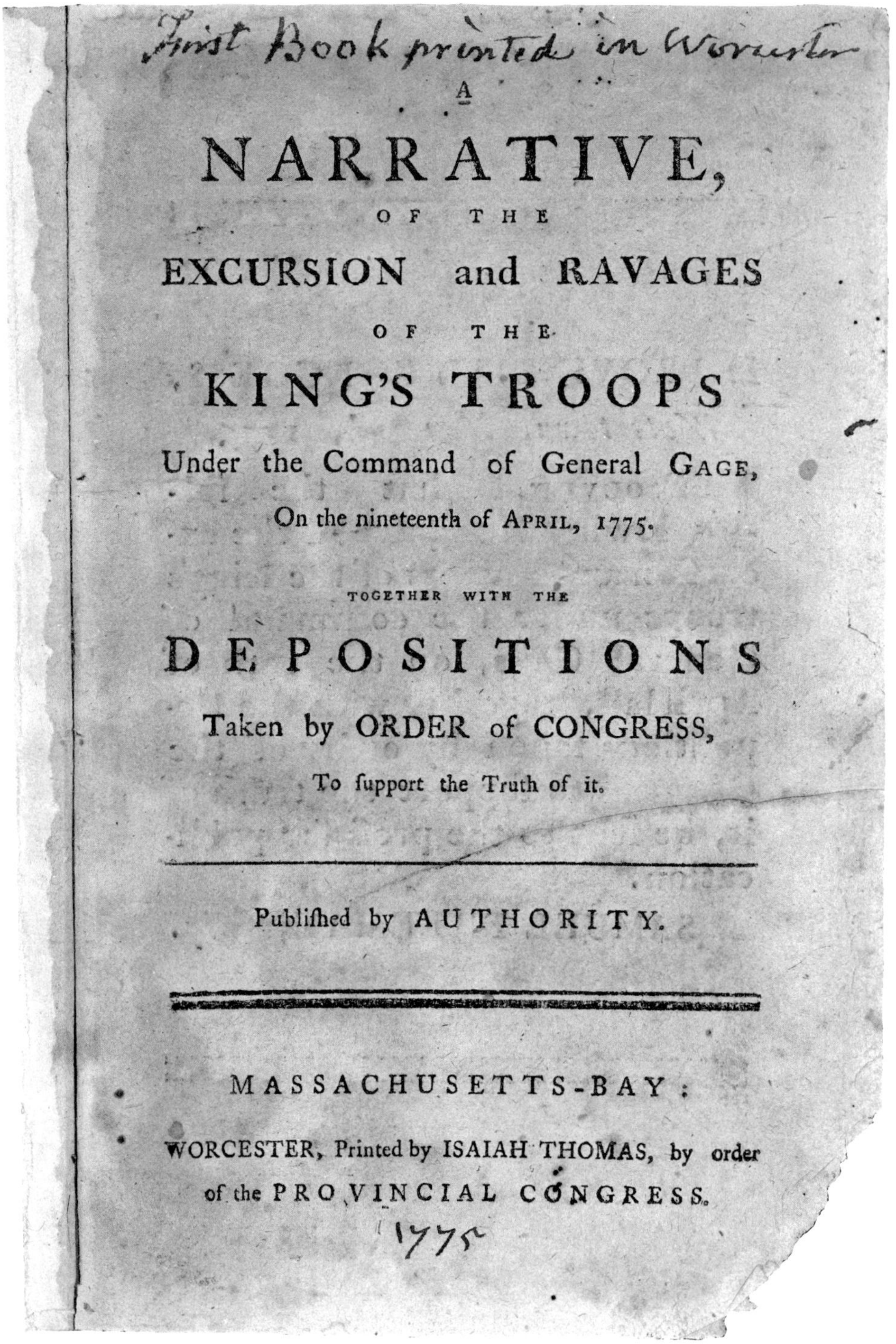

First Book printed in Worcester

A
NARRATIVE,

OF THE

EXCURSION and RAVAGES

OF THE

KING'S TROOPS

Under the Command of General GAGE,

On the nineteenth of APRIL, 1775.

TOGETHER WITH THE

DEPOSITIONS

Taken by ORDER of CONGRESS,

To support the Truth of it.

Published by AUTHORITY.

MASSACHUSETTS-BAY:

WORCESTER, Printed by ISAIAH THOMAS, by order
of the PROVINCIAL CONGRESS.

1775

149. An American account of British 'atrocities' at Lexington and Concord

England and her colonies had been at war for more than a year before the Declaration of Independence. On April 18, 1775, Gen. Thomas Gage had ordered seven hundred men toward Concord, a few miles inland from Boston, to seize a cache of patriot arms and ammunition. Patriot dispatch riders Paul Revere, William Dawes, and Samuel Prescott alerted the countryside. Militiamen attempted to stop Gage's troops at Lexington, five miles from Concord, but failed. Marching on to Concord, the British fought a minor skirmish and then began to head back to Boston, but four thousand militiamen had gathered behind stone fences and trees along the route. The Americans attacked the redcoats savagely, and only the arrival of reinforcements saved the British from total slaughter.

Before the news from Massachusetts had been carried a hundred miles, patriots followed Lexington and Concord with a series of military strikes up and down the coast. When the Continental Congress reconvened in May 1775, it found itself in the middle of a war the direction of which would be its principal function for the next twelve months.

149

A Narrative of the Excursion and Ravages of the King's Troops

Worcester, 1775. Adams 181. Evans 14269.

This pamphlet, prepared for the Massachusetts Provincial Congress, was the first imprint issued by Isaiah Thomas in Worcester, Massachusetts, as noted by the printer on the title page. It consists of eyewitness accounts of the battles of Lexington and Concord. These depositions allege that the British troops fired the first shots and that the Americans were merely defending themselves. A list of the dead, wounded, and missing appears at the end of the pamphlet.

150

The Massachusetts Spy or, American Oracle of Liberty, Vol. V, Number 219

Worcester, May 3, 1775.

This issue of Isaiah Thomas's *Massachusetts Spy*, which contains an account of the battles of Lexington and Concord, was the first to be printed in Worcester. The events of April 1775 had forced him to abandon Boston for safety's sake and to set up his press in Worcester. Thomas also published several other magazines and papers, and after the war turned his energies to books, of which the most famous were his children's books. By 1802 he had become wealthy and he devoted the rest of his life to scholarship. His personal library furnished the source material for the *History of Printing in America* (1810). Realizing the need for a national society for the preservation and study of the materials of American history, he founded the American Antiquarian Society in 1812.

151

A Circumstantial Account of an Attack that Happened on the 19th of April 1775, on His Majesty's Troops

[Boston, 1775.] Evans 13869.

The British version of the events leading to and including the battles at Lexington and Concord is presented in this broadside. The account carefully emphasizes that the Americans fired their guns first and that they committed atrocities such as scalping and ambushing. The broadside concludes that the entire 'unfortunate affair' would not have happened had the 'country People' not fired on the British troops.

152

The Seat of War, in New England, by an American Volunteer

London, 1775. Nebenzahl 6.

This map provides an overview of the area where the Revolution first broke out. Along the major roads, American troops are seen heading for Boston. At the far left (Worcester County), General Washington's troops are depicted marching along the road toward Boston. New Hampshire regulars and Connecticut troops are also clearly rendered. Their destination is Boston where they would engage in the Battle of Bunker Hill. The inset on the lower right illustrates this engagement by showing Charlestown in flames and the English forces squaring off against the American forces.

153   ELISHA RICH (1740–1804?)

[A Poem] On the Bloody Engagement that was Fought on Bunker's Hill

[Chelmsford, 1775.] Evans 14426.

On June 17, 1775, General Gage, the commander of the British troops in Boston, detached a large assault force from Boston to oust the Americans from a fortification they had begun to build on Breed's Hill (mistakenly called Bunker Hill) across the Charles River. The garrison of 1,600 Americans was forced to withdraw, but at a cost of 1,054 British casualties, many of them officers. The struggle was celebrated in this poem written by Elisha Rich.

154

A Plan of Boston and its Environs Shewing the True Situation of His Majesty's Army. And Also Those of the Rebels

London, 1776. Nebenzahl 16.

This map shows Boston and the surrounding area four months after Lexington and Concord. The British controlled the town of Boston itself, but Cambridge was the headquarters of the rebels. Bunker Hill is clearly shown next to General Howe's camp north of Charlestown, and the spot where Howe landed his troops on June 17 is also indicated just east of Charlestown. Troops are indicated by lines of symbolic tents, and a convenient reference table for landmarks is provided to the right of the map. Note that although the town had been secured, the countryside had not. Howe later wrote home describing the impossibility of ever occupying the entire country.

155

A Proclamation for the Public Thanksgiving

Watertown, 1775. Evans 14199.

Although proclamations for public thanksgivings were usually made by colonial governors, this one was issued by the Massachusetts Council in Watertown. The familiar litany of British abuses is given at the top of the broadside. This is followed by a prayer that God would bless the new country, its leaders, Congress, and the armies, and preserve America's mission by making the country 'Emanuel's Land.' Note the inscription 'God save the People' rather than 'God save the King' at the bottom.

156   ELISHA RICH (1740–1804?)

A Poem on the Late Distress of the Town of Boston

Chelmsford, Massachusetts, 1776. Evans 15061. Gift of Matt B. Jones, 1933.

The evacuation of Boston by the British army on March 17, 1776, is celebrated in this poem by Elisha Rich, whose initials may be found in the last verse. The poem alludes to the Stamp Act, the closing of the port of Boston, and the Battle of Bunker Hill. The last nine stanzas are an impassioned plea to Ameri-

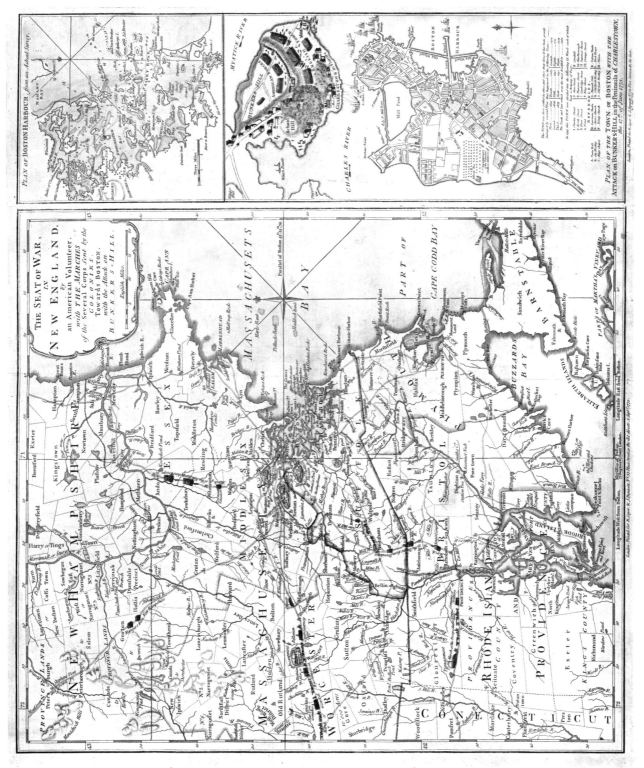

152. A map of the first battles of the American Revolution

A POEM

On the late distress of the
TOWN OF
BOSTON

With some Remarks of the sudden Flight of the Ministerial Troops, after plundering and Destroying the Property of the Worthy Inhabitants they left the town in the greatest confusion imaginable, not allowing themselves time to take with them great part of their Warlike Stores, In short, they fled like Murderers pursued by the Hand of Justice.

COME shout Americans with Joy,
And let God's praise your tongues employ,
Who did our foes designs destroy,
That would our Liberties annoy.

Your officers and soldiers brave,
By God's kind hand, your land doth save,
While britons seeking to inslave,
Sink deeper down into their grave.

Britanna's glory once was high,
While she sought peace and liberty;
Her fame around the earth did fly,
And King's her greatness did envy.

She might still greater glory see:
Her Prince, sons of rebels been,
Had she have let her Sons been free,
And never crown'd the bramble-tree.

This bramble so in pride did rise,
So void of love and pitying eyes,
He would not hear the oppressed crys,
But did their humble suits despise.

My pow'r unlimitted, I say
Shall over the whole Realm bear sway:
My taxing power they shall obey,
Through the whole North-America.

My Parliament espouse my cause,
Men of true merit and applause;
My Commoners enforce my laws,
And from my help there's few withdraws:

Tall Cedars in America,
Shall bend their lofty tops to me,
And from taxes shall not be free,
Yet represented here shan't be.

Americans could not endure
To fall beneath a tyrant's power;
And tho' his wrath would them devour,
Yet they submit not for one hour.

While they request superior aid;
They do refuse the bramble shade,
And while his laws are not obey'd,
They of his frowns are not afraid.

His wrath doth first on Boston fall;
He stops our Ports and Harbour's all,
Then for his bloody troops doth call
For to inslave or murder all.

Thus stoping our Commerce and trade,
The Town of BOSTON they invade,
And in her streets they do parade,
Till it a den of thieves is made.

Her Liberty for to confound,
With fleets and armies her surround;
With trenches they threw up her ground,
While tyrants Drums and Trumpets sound.

In Boston they dominion bare,
It's owners treasure they don't spare,
But like blood-hounds that hungry were,
They rob and pillage every where.

This Town their garrison they make,
While it's true owner's hearts do ake:
At length the Town, they must forsake,
To other Town's for safety take.

Before hostilitie's commenc't,
They have the Town for their defence,
Their Cannon mounted to dispence,
Destruction to Americans.

When they this Town had fortified,
With strong defence on every side:
There's now no Bridle to their pride,
They think none can their force abide.

They then begin their murderous theme,
Well pleas'd with their curs't plot they seem,
Their victory now a pleasing dream,
Till justice o'rthrows their scheme.

Americans this murder see,
And could no longer silent be,
But with one mind and heart agree,
To set unhappy Boston free.

In Seventy-Five this war began,
With fighting while the year was run,
With Cannon, bayonet and Gun,
While blood on either side did run.

Our Colonies unite as one,
Commanded by brave WASHINGTON,
Who to our help together run,
Whose braved swords and armour shone.

Brave WASHINGTON is valiant found,
His Men our tyrant foes surround,
Their cruel Plot he doth confound,
And is at last with victory crown'd.

Our foes through fear did melt away,
To see our Fort's rise night and day;
The Admiral to How did say,
These Rebels Drive, or I'll not stay.

These bloody Troops to mem'ry call,
How they on Bunker's Hill did fall;
They have no courage left at all,
They run away Torries and all.

They quit their Fort on Bunker's Hill,
Tho' bitterly against their will,
They fear to stay, least they see hell,
Adue, Boston, Boston farewell.

On Seventeenth of March they flee,
Since there they could no safety see;
Left Boston to it's owner's free,
And trust the mercy of the sea.

With shame the City they resign'd,
And left much of their store's behind,
Nor could they in our Harbour find,
A shelter from the stormy wind.

God grant these troops may never more,
Have footing on New-England shore,
To lay her Sons in bloody gore,
To set up an oppressive pow'r.

By sea they oft defeated were,
Before their transports came a shore,
And lost much of their warlike hore,
And many were laid in their gore.

Britanna now consider well,
Thy forces that us'd to excel,
By sad defeats doth plainly tell,
The cause they'r in is black as hell.

By slaughter in America,
Doth not blood's gilt upon the lay,
Then bid farewel to peace for aye,
Unless blood clenses, blood's gilt away.

Blood's gilt doth call for blood again,
Nought else can wash away it's stain,
If than thy murderer's are not slain,
You draw your swords for war in vain.

You that in Boston dwellers were,
And have been scattered here and there,
How doth your hearts rejoice to hear,
Your City of those murderer's clear.

Give glory to the Lord most high,
Who did defeat thine enemy,
That so few of thy son's did die,
Or went into captivity.

Some that were neighbour's once to you,
That joined with this bloody crew,
Through fear and shame, are now withdrew,
And those that stay'd, their deeds may rue.

Should you again your Lord posess,
And God should you increase and bless:
Avoid all luxerous excess,
Lest God bring still greater distress.

Americans consider all,
What fate on British tyrants fall,
And pattern not by them at all,
Lest you in vain for helpers call.

While you behold God's wond'rous hand,
In guarding thee by sea and land:
Trust in his Name and as a friend,
He will thy glorious cause defend.

All covetous desires disdain,
Nor judge amiss for lukers gain,
But lovers of true peace remain,
And you'll not find God's promise vain.

Oppress not in Religion still;
Tax none to Priest's against their will,
For this will peace and friendship kill,
And the whole state with tumult fill.

For as in things of God we see,
Men's conscience's are wholly free,
True sons of peace cannot agree,
That worldly masterhip should be.

Christ's Kingdom here hath true defence,
From the true Gospel influence:
Nor needs it fines or prisonments,
Or robing to bear it's expence.

Can Patriots for Liberty,
Against a civil tyrants cry,
And not give equal Liberty,
To ev'ry diff'rent sectary.

Then let America be free,
And love true peace and Liberty;
That God our lasting friend may be,
To the latest posterity.

If these afflictions should be blest
And many should releave th' oppress,
That we in God may find true rest,
Thy friend E. R. hath his request.

CHELMSFORD: Printed and Sold at N. Coverly's Printing-Office   Where may be had, Verses by the Groze or Dozen, M,DCCLXXVI.

156. A poem celebrating the evacuation of Boston by the British army on March 17, 1776

cans not to commit the sins of the British Government when they undertake self-government. The woodcut on this broadside had been used previously on a broadside ballad, also written by Rich, which celebrated the skirmish at the Light House in 1775. Hence the iconography of the boat, cannon, and lighthouse.

WASHINGTON AND THE ARMY

In June 1775 the Continental Congress appointed George Washington as commander-in-chief of the new continental army. By European standards, the American army was no match for the British, who were trained, disciplined, and thoroughly versed in the formalized art of war, as practiced in Europe. But the war was being waged in America where the colonists had learned from the Indians how to fight. The war was a struggle for survival to be fought with cunning and resourcefulness. Fighting on and defending their own territory potentially gave the Americans an advantage, but only if the troops could be forged into a disciplined army. Washington's tasks were therefore enormous. He had to organize supplies, secure trustworthy officers, recruit and drill his troops, instill habits of obedience, alleviate sectional and ethnic animosities, and deal with the loyalists. Already by the end of 1776, Washington's success as a leader was such that he was celebrated in ballads and on the stage as a popular American hero.

157

The Theatre of War in North America

Engraving, London, 1776. Bequest of John W. Farwell, 1943.

This English map of North America depicts the colonies in 1776. The Province of Quebec extended down to the Ohio River and included large expanses of territory previously claimed by the thirteen rebellious colonies. The extension of Quebec into this area had been proclaimed by one of those parliamentary acts of 1774 which the colonists described as 'Intolerable.'

158

For the Encouragement of Those that Shall Inlist in the Continental Army

[Boston, 1776.] Evans 14870.

To encourage enlistments in the continental army, Congress offered material inducements such as those listed on this broadside. In addition to a twenty-dollar bounty and an assortment of clothing, each man who enlisted for the duration of the war as a noncommissioned officer or private soldier (or his survivor) was to receive one hundred acres of land.

159

In Congress. December 30, 1776

Baltimore, 1776. Evans 15178. Gift of Frank S. Streeter, 1970.

In order to feed a desperate army, Congress prohibited the exportation of certain foodstuffs. This broadside, printed in Baltimore, where Congress met after Philadelphia was seized, asks the executive powers in the individual states to see that the resolution be obeyed.

160   THOMAS HANSON (d. 1777)

The Prussian Evolutions in Actual Engagements

Philadelphia, [1775]. Evans 14098.

The author of this book of drill instructions is described on the title page as the 'Adjutant to the 2d Battalion. And Teacher of part of the American Militia.' It was used by the Pennsylvania militia for a time and is a precursor of von Steuben's guides. The author died in battle August 13, 1777.

161 FRIEDRICH WILHELM AUGUST HEINRICH FERDINAND VON STEUBEN (1730-1794)

Regulations for the Order and Discipline of the Troops of the United States

Philadelphia, 1779. Evans 16627. Gift of Charles H. Banister, 1931.

Baron von Steuben was a professional soldier and military expert from Magdeburg, Germany, who became the inspector general of the continental army. He brought to Washington's staff sophisticated training that was unknown in either the French or British armies at that time. Upon arriving in America in December 1777 he was placed in charge of training the army by Washington. Von Steuben spoke little English and there was no time to prepare and publish a complete new drill manual, so he wrote his drill instructions in brief installments, which were then translated into English and issued to the regiments as the drills progressed. During the winter of 1778-1779, he prepared this book which contains the essentials of military instruction and procedure adapted to the needs of Americans. The book is opened to instructions on the formation of a company and regiment and reference is made to Plate I, which is unfolded.

162 CHRISTIAN GULLAGER (1759-1826)

Portrait of John May 1743-1812

Oil painting, 1789. Bequest of Mary Davenport May and Charlotte Augusta May, 1874.

John May was a participant in the Boston Tea Party and later a colonel of the First Regiment of the Bos-

ton militia during the Revolution. This painting was done from life by Christian Gullager, a Dane who emigrated to America between 1782 and 1786. His best-known work is a portrait of George Washington, but this painting of May captures a certain arrogant pride that would have escaped many artists.

163

Portrait of William Henshaw (1735-1820)

Oil painting, ca. 1800. Bequest of Harriet E. Henshaw, 1896.

By the time of the Revolution, William Henshaw was an experienced soldier who served under Lord Jeffrey Amherst against the French in 1759. An ardent patriot, he fought in the American Revolution as lieutenant colonel in the continental army. George Washington, who recognized Henshaw's military skills, had personally requested that Henshaw accept the commission.

164 THOMAS EARLE (1737-1819)

Silver Mounted Firelock Gun

Bequest of Harriet E. Henshaw, 1896.

This musket was manufactured in 1773 by Thomas Earle, a master American gunsmith noted for his mechanical skill and ingenuity. He made the weapon for Col. William Henshaw (1735-1820), who subsequently used it in the American Revolution. George Washington observed the gun in battle and became such an admirer of it that he ordered one of the same pattern made for himself.

165

Colony of New Hampshire. In Committee of Safety, April 12th, 1776

[Portsmouth, 1776.] Evans 14904.

This New Hampshire broadside reprints the resolution of the Continental Congress which sought to

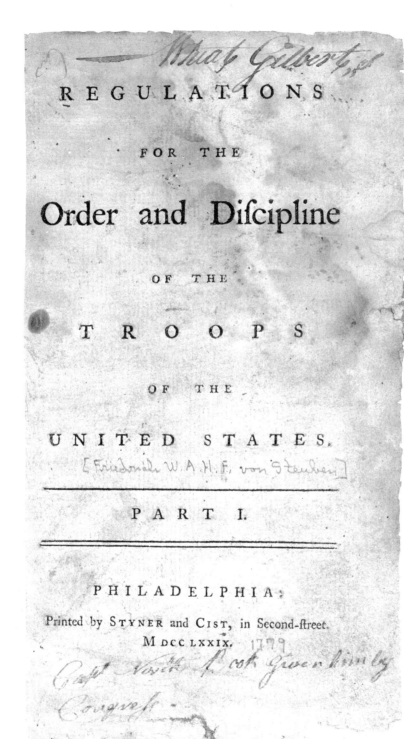

REGULATIONS

FOR THE

Order and Discipline

OF THE

TROOPS

OF THE

UNITED STATES.

[Friedrich W. A. H. F. von Steuben]

PART I.

PHILADELPHIA:

Printed by Styner and Cist, in Second-street.
MDCCLXXIX.

161. Von Steuben's drill manual for the Continental Army

162. Christian Gullager's portrait of Col. John May of the Boston militia

identify and disarm the loyalists. The New Hampshire Committee of Safety sent a declaration to each town to be signed by those willing to join their 'American Brethren, in defending the Lives, Liberties, and Properties of the Inhabitants of the United Colonies' against the 'Hostile Proceedings of the British Fleets, and Armies.'

166

By His Excellency George Washington, Esq; General, and Commander in Chief, of all the Forces of the United States of America. Proclamation

Philadelphia, [1777]. Evans 15632.

Washington became increasingly alarmed over the number of people who had become loyalists when confronted with the armed might of the British forces. Thus he issued this proclamation which commanded that anyone who had sworn allegiance to, or who had accepted protection from General Howe, take an oath of allegiance to the United States of America. Those who would not or could not do so, he asked to 'withdraw themselves and families within the enemy lines.' Anyone who refused to comply with either of these requests, he declared, would be treated as a common enemy of the United States.

167 JONATHAN MITCHELL SEWALL (1748–1808)

A New Song

No place, [1776]. Evans 14918.

Written by Sewall, a lawyer and poet of Portsmouth, New Hampshire, this patriotic song praising Washington is typical of dozens of poems and ballads written during the Revolution. It is not unlike those printed during the French and Indian War. Indeed this one is sung to the tune of the 'British Grenadier,' which the Americans had sung with great pride during that struggle. Now, however, Washington has taken the place of George III, and America the place of Britain.

168 JOHN LEACOCK

The Fall of British Tyranny: or, American Liberty Triumphant

Philadelphia, 1776. Evans 14823.

Leacock was a coroner and an innkeeper in Philadelphia who occasionally wrote plays, such as this satire on the English, their corrupt society and manners, and their arbitrary government. The play was performed by amateurs in Philadelphia in 1776, and General Washington appears among the 'dramatis personae.' Other characters in the play include Lord Wisdom (William Pitt), Lord Patriot (John Wilkes), Bold Irishman (Edmund Burke), and Lord Boston (General Gage). The action begins with imaginary events in England before the Revolution, continues with the battles about Boston, and ends with the evacuation of that city by the British and a ringing cry for 'Independence!'

The future looked bleak for Americans in the winter of 1776–1777, but Washington boosted the morale of the citizenry by executing a pair of daring raids against the British at Trenton and Princeton. During the following summer Gen. John Burgoyne launched a British offensive from Canada, but Horatio Gates and Benedict Arnold stubbornly resisted and forced the British commander to surrender at Saratoga in October 1777.

Meanwhile Washington's army spent the winter of 1777–1778 at Valley Forge. The successes of Gates at Saratoga, John Paul Jones on the high seas, and George Rogers Clark in the Ohio country, however, helped persuade the French to enter the war on the American side. At the same time, Washington's forces survived the bitter winter and became stronger for the experience.

The army's newfound strength came at an opportune time, for during the year following Saratoga, the British prepared for an offensive against the South. Lord Cornwallis, the commander of the southern forces, was successful in South Carolina, but when he pushed northward he encountered fierce American resistance. Accordingly, in 1781 he withdrew his overextended army to Yorktown where he surrendered to a combined Franco-American army on October 17, 1781.

The defeat at Yorktown persuaded the British to begin peace negotiations, and in early 1783 a treaty was signed at Paris which officially ended hostilities and recognized American independence.

169

A Plan of the City of New York & its Environs

London, [1776].

This map was dedicated to General Gage, the 'Commander in Chief of his Majesty's Forces in North America.' Drawn before the British took the city in November 1776, it is a skillfully rendered view of New York in 1775. A reference guide to landmarks and buildings is provided at the bottom, and a brief narrative of the colony's history is given at the lower left. Cities such as New York, Philadelphia, and Boston fell easily to the British, but America was primarily an agrarian country (most of Manhattan was farmland), and so such victories in the long run accomplished little for the British.

170 JOSIAH PARKER (1751–1810)

Letter, October 1777

Manuscript, U.S. Revolution Collection.

Parker, a colonel in the Fifth Virginia regiment, won plaudits for his actions in the battles of Trenton, Princeton, and Brandywine. This letter was written to John Page, lieutenant governor of Virginia, after the victory in the Battle of Saratoga, and, as the opening lines indicate, Parker was euphoric. He describes the surrender of Burgoyne to 'the High and Mighty States of America,' and then proceeds to present an account of the battle. Saratoga was a turning point in the war, for with that victory the Americans were able to convince the French that they had a chance to win. As a result, in February 1778 the United States and France agreed to a treaty of friendship and alliance, and France officially joined the American struggle for independence by declaring war on Britain.

171

An Address of the Congress to the Inhabitants of the United States of America

Boston, [1778]. Evans 16099.

Periodically during the war, Congress felt obliged to

172. John Paul Jones and the *Bon Homme Richard* in action against the British navy

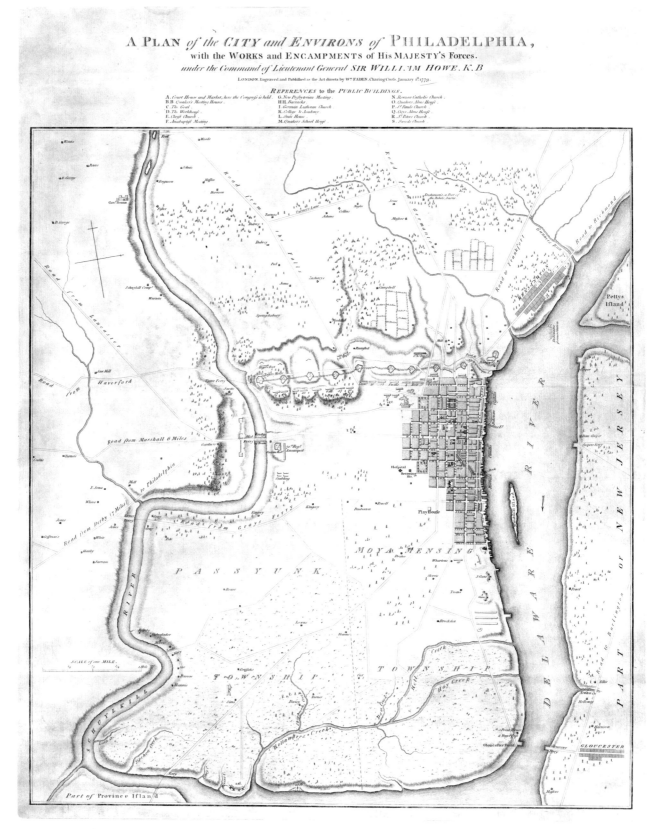

A PLAN of the CITY and ENVIRONS of PHILADELPHIA,
with the WORKS and ENCAMPMENTS of His MAJESTY'S Forces.
under the Command of Lieutenant General SIR WILLIAM HOWE, K.B

LONDON. Engraved and Published as the Act directs by Wᵐ FADEN, Charing Cross, January 1ˢᵗ 1779.

REFERENCES to the PUBLIC BUILDINGS.

A. Court House and Market, here the Congress is held.
B.B. Quakers Meeting House.
C. The Goal.
D. The Workhouse.
F. Christ Church.
V. Anabaptist Meeting.

G. New Presbyterian Meeting.
H.H. Barracks.
I. German Lutheran Church.
K. College & Academy.
L. State House.
M. Quakers School House.

N. Roman Catholic Church.
O. Quakers Alms House.
P. Sᵗ Pauls Church.
Q. Cyes Alms House.
R. Sᵗ Pters Church.
S. Swedes Church.

174. Philadelphia in 1779

rekindle patriotic spirit by listing the evils the British had wrought upon America. This broadside reiterated the causes of the war and added further reasons that had come to light during the course of the conflict. It described the British side as 'fraud and violence labouring in the service of despotism,' and the American side as 'virtue and fortitude supporting the rights of human nature.' The statement encouraged the reader to support the war effort even if it meant additional hardships, for soon 'the full tide of wealth will flow in upon your shores, free from the arbitrary impositions of those, whose interest, and whose declared policy it was, to check your growth.'

172 JOHN BOYDELL

The Memorable Engagement of . . . the Serapis, *with* . . . *the* Bon Homme Richard

Engraving, London, 1780. Bequest of Charles H. Taylor, 1948.

This print depicts the naval engagement of the *Bon Homme Richard*, commanded by John Paul Jones, and the *Serapis*, captained by Sir Richard Pearson. Jones had already made his reputation with the daring exploits of the *Ranger*, a sloop which he used to make commando raids in the British Isles and to capture seven English prizes. Given a French ship, rechristened by Jones as the *Bon Homme Richard*, he encountered the *Serapis* in September 1779. Jones's ship was outclassed, but by clever close maneuvering he lessened the odds against him and fought a three-hour battle which ranks as one of the most desperate and bloody engagements in naval history. The *Richard* eventually won mainly because of the courage and tenacity of Jones. This and other achievements not only encouraged Americans at home, but helped persuade the French to continue their support of the rebels.

173 NATHANAEL GREENE (1742–1786)

Letter, January 5, 1778

Manuscript, Nathanael Greene Papers.

Greene, a Revolutionary general from Rhode Island, took part in the siege of Boston, the Battle of New York, the Battle of White Plains, Washington's Christmastime triumph at Trenton in 1776, and a number of skirmishes with the British. He also participated in the Battle of Brandywine where his skillful disposition of troops insured the safe withdrawal of the army and saved the artillery. In November 1777 Greene was directed to try to hold the forts on the Delaware, but was unable to do so and returned with his troops to the main army, then going into winter quarters at Valley Forge. This letter, dated January 5, 1778, is from the camp at Valley Forge. Addressed to Greene's friend Samuel Ward (1756–1832), it opens with a discussion of the ineptitude of Congress and the administration of the war. Later on, Greene remarks on the wretched conditions at Valley Forge and praises the troops. In 1780–1781 Greene would conduct a series of successful campaigns against General Cornwallis in the South.

174

A Plan of the City and Environs of Philadelphia, with the Works and Encampments of His Majesty's Forces

Engraving, London, 1779. Nebenzahl 128.

This engraved map shows the locations of the fortifications and the camps of the British, who held Philadelphia from September 1777 to the winter of 1779–1780. The fortifications isolated the city from the north as the rivers did on the east, south, and west.

175

The Sentiments of an American Woman

Philadelphia, 1780. Evans 16992.

Although several women like Molly Pitcher and Margaret Corbin actually fought in the Revolution, most females expressed their patriotism in quieter, more symbolic gestures. Many wore homespun, refused to drink imported tea, and renounced European finery. The reverse of this broadside suggests a very practical plan by which American women could put in effect their noble sentiments. They could donate cash to a fund which George Washington would administer 'in the manner he shall judge most advantageous to the Soldiery.' The American women hoped that the money would be used 'to render the condition of the Soldier more pleasant' and not be used to buy clothing and arms.

176

A Sketch of the Operations before Charleston the Capital of South Carolina 1780

Engraving, [Trenton, 1785]. Wheat and Brun 595.

Following their defeat at Saratoga, the British prepared for another offensive, this time aimed at the South. The campaign began when Lord Cornwallis captured Charleston and occupied most of South Carolina in late 1778 and early 1779. This map shows Charleston in 1780 with the British troops under the command of Sir Henry Clinton, just before the Americans attempted unsuccessfully to retake South Carolina.

177

A Sketch of the Battle of Camden in South Carolina Aug. 16, 1780

Engraving, [London, 1780?]. Nebenzahl 89.

After the Americans failed to regain Charleston, Lord Cornwallis soundly defeated the American army at Camden in August 1780. When Cornwallis attempted to push further north, the Americans, under the command of General Greene, rebuffed him. The British army also suffered severe losses at the Battle of Guilford Court House, in North Carolina. Seriously weakened as a result, Cornwallis withdrew his army to Yorktown in tidewater Virginia, where he hoped to be evacuated by the British fleet.

178

Plan of the Siege of York Town in Virginia

Engraving, London, 1787. Nebenzahl 197.

When Cornwallis withdrew his army to Yorktown he hoped to be evacuated by the British fleet, but on his arrival he found the French navy anchored offshore instead. Meanwhile, Washington and the French commanders had marched their combined Franco-American army down from the north. Thus checkmated by hostile sea and land forces, as this map clearly indicates, Cornwallis had no alternative but to surrender on October 17, 1781. The American countryside had proven to be too vast, the population too deeply committed to resistance, and the costs of supporting an army three thousand miles away too expensive. The debacle at Yorktown was the last action of the war. Peace negotiations began in late 1781.

179

Weatherwise's Town and Country Almanack for the Year of Our Lord, 1782

Boston, [1781]. Evans 17354.

This almanac, printed shortly after the surrender of Cornwallis at Yorktown, is decorated with a copperplate engraving celebrating the end of the War for Independence. This complex print shows 'America' on the right and a dejected 'Britannia' on the left. In the background is New York, where Benedict Arnold, the traitor to his country, is depicted from a gallows. Actually, Arnold fled to England where he spent the rest of his life.

180

A Poem, Spoken Extempore, by a Young Lady, on . . . the Surrender of York-Town

[Boston, 1782.] Bristol 5572. MP 44247.

THE SENTIMENTS of an
AMERICAN WOMAN.

ON the commencement of actual war, the Women of America manifested a firm refolution to contribute as much as could depend on them, to the deliverance of their country. Animated by the pureft patriotifm, they are fenfible of forrow at this day, in not offering more than barren wifhes for the fuccefs of fo glorious a Revolution. They afpire to render themfelves more really ufeful; and this fentiment is univerfal from the north to the fouth of the Thirteen United States. Our ambition is kindled by the fame of thofe heroines of antiquity, who have rendered their fex illuftrious, and have proved to the univerfe, that, if the weaknefs of our Conftitution, if opinion and manners did not forbid us to march to glory by the fame paths as the Men, we fhould at leaft equal, and fometimes furpafs them in our love for the public good. I glory in all that which my fex has done great and commendable. I call to mind with enthufiafm and with admiration, all thofe acts of courage, of conftancy and patriotifm, which hiftory has tranfmitted to us: The people favoured by Heaven, preferved from deftruction by the virtues, the zeal and the refolution of Deborah, of Judith, of Efther! The fortitude of the mother of the Macchabees, in giving up her fons to die before her eyes: Rome faved from the fury of a victorious enemy by the efforts of Volumnia, and other Roman Ladies: So many famous fieges where the Women have been feen forgeting the weaknefs of their fex, building new walls, digging trenches with their feeble hands, furnifhing arms to their defenders, they themfelves darting the miffile weapons on the enemy, refigning the ornaments of their apparel, and their fortune, to fill the public treafury, and to haften the deliverance of their country; burying themfelves under its ruins; throwing themfelves into the flames rather than fubmit to the difgrace of humiliation before a proud enemy.

Born for liberty, difdaining to bear the irons of a tyrannic Government, we affociate ourfelves to the grandeur of thofe Sovereigns, cherifhed and revered, who have held with fo much fplendour the fcepter of the greateft States, The Batildas, the Elizabeths, the Maries, the Catharines, who have extended the empire of liberty, and contented to reign by fweetnefs and juftice, have broken the chains of flavery, forged by tyrants in the times of ignorance and barbarity. The Spanifh Women, do they not make, at this moment, the moft patriotic facrifices, to encreafe the means of victory in the hands of their Sovereign. He is a friend to the French Nation. They are our allies. We call to mind, doubly interefted, that it was a French Maid who kindled up amongft her fellow-citizens, the flame of patriotifm buried under long misfortunes: It was the Maid of Orleans who drove from the kingdom of France the anceftors of thofe fame Britifh, whofe odious yoke we have juft fhaken off; and whom it is neceffary that we drive from this Continent.

But I muft limit myfelf to the recollection of this fmall number of atchievements. Who knows if perfons difpofed to cenfure, and fometimes too feverely with regard to us, may not difapprove our appearing acquainted even with the actions of which our fex boafts? We are at leaft certain, that he cannot be a good citizen who will not applaud our efforts for the relief of the armies which defend our lives, our poffeffions, our liberty? The fituation of our foldiery has been reprefented to me; the evils infeparable from war, and the firm and generous fpirit which has enabled them to fupport thefe. But it has been faid, that they may apprehend, that, in the courfe of a long war, the view of their diftreffes may be loft, and their fervices be forgotten. Forgotten! never; I can anfwer in the name of all my fex. Brave Americans, your difinterestednefs, your courage, and your conftancy will always be dear to America, as long as fhe fhall preferve her virtue.

We know that at a diftance from the theatre of war, if we enjoy any tranquility, it is the fruit of your watchings, your labours, your dangers. If I live happy in the midft of my family; if my hufband cultivates his field, and reaps his harveft in peace; if, furrounded with my children, I myfelf nourifh the youngeft, and prefs it to my bofom, without being affraid of feeing myfelf feparated from it, by a ferocious enemy; if the houfe in which we dwell; if our barns, our orchards are fafe at the prefent time from the hands of thofe incendiaries, it is to you that we owe it. And fhall we hefitate to evidence to you our gratitude? Shall we hefitate to wear a cloathing more fimple; hair dreffed lefs elegant, while at the price of this fmall privation, we fhall deferve your benedictions. Who, amongft us, will not renounce with the higheft pleafure, thofe vain ornaments, when fhe fhall confider that the valiant defenders of America will be able to draw fome advantage from the money which fhe may have laid out in thefe; that they will be better defended from the rigours of the feafons, that after their painful toils, they will receive fome extraordinary and unexpected relief; that thefe prefents will perhaps be valued by them at a greater price, when they will have it in their power to fay: *This is the offering of the Ladies.* The time is arrived to difplay the fame fentiments which animated us at the beginning of the Revolution, when we renounced the ufe of teas, however agreeable to our tafte, rather than receive them from our perfecutors; when we made it appear to them that we placed former neceffaries in the rank of fuperfluities, when our liberty was interefted; when our republican and laborious hands fpun the flax, prepared the linen intended for the ufe of our foldiers; when exiles and fugitives we fupported with courage all the evils which are the concomitants of war. Let us not lofe a moment; let us be engaged to offer the homage of our gratitude at the altar of military valour, and you, our brave deliverers, while mercenary flaves combat to caufe you to fhare with them, the irons with which they are loaded, receive with a free hand our offering, the pureft which can be prefented to your virtue,

BY AN AMERICAN WOMAN.

175. An American woman's views on the War

IDEAS, relative to the manner of forwarding to the American Soldiers, the Presents of the American Women.

ALL plans are eligible, when doing good is the object; there is however one more preferable; and when the operation is extensive, we cannot give it too much uniformity. On the other side, the wants of our army do not permit the slowness of an ordinary path. It is not in one month, nor in eight days, that we would releve our soldiery. It is immediately; and our impatience does not permit us to proceed by the long circuity of collectors, receivers and treasurers. As my idea with regard to this, have been approved by some Ladies of my friends, I will explain them here; every other person will not be less at liberty to prepare and to adopt a different plan.

1st. All Women and Girls will be received without exception, to present their patriotic offering; and, as it is absolutely voluntary, every one will regulate it according to her ability, and her disposition. The shilling offered by the Widow or the young Girl, will be received as well as the most considerable sums presented by the Women who have the happiness to join to their patriotism, greater means to be useful.

2d. A Lady chosen by the others in each county, shall be the Treasuress; and to render her task more simple, and more easy, she will not receive but determinate sums, in a round number, from twenty hard dollars to any greater sum. The exchange forty dollars in paper for one dollar in specie.

It is hoped that there will not be one Woman who will not with pleasure charge herself with the embarrassment which will attend so honorable an operation.

3d. The Women who shall not be in a condition to send twenty dollars in specie, or above, will join in as great a number as will be necessary to make this or any greater sum, and one amongst them will carry it, or cause it to be sent to the Treasuress.

4th. The Treasuress of the county will receive the money, and will keep a register, writing the sums in her book, and causing it to be signed at the side of the whole by the person who has presented it.

5th. When several Women shall join together to make a total sum of twenty dollars or more, she amongst them who shall have the charge to carry it to the Treasuress, will make mention of all their names on the register, if her associates shall have so directed her; those whose choice it shall be, will have the liberty to remain unknown.

6th. As soon as the Treasuress of the county shall judge, that the sums which she shall have received, deserve to be sent to their destination, she will cause them to be presented with the lists, to the wife of the Governor or President of the State, who will be the Treasuress-General of the State; and she will cause it to be set down in her register, and have it sent to Mistress Washington. If the Governor or President are unmarried, all will address themselves to the wife of the Vice-President, if there is one, or of the Chief-Justice, &c.

7th. Women settled in the distant parts of the country, and not chusing for any particular reason as for the sake of greater expedition, to remit their Capital to the Treasuress, may send it directly to the wife of the Governor, or President, &c. or to Mistress Washington, who, if she shall judge necessary, will in a short answer to the sender, acquaint her with the reception of it.

8th. As Mrs. Washington may be absent from the camp when the greater part of the banks shall be sent there, the American Women considering, that General Washington is the Father and Friend of the Soldiery; that he is himself, the first Soldier of the Republic, and that their offering will be received at its destination, as soon as it shall have come to his hands, they will pray him, to take the charge of receiving it, in the absence of Mrs. Washington.

9th. General Washington will dispose of this fund in the manner that he shall judge most advantageous to the Soldiery. The American Women desire only that it may not be considered as to be employed, to procure to the army, the objects of subsistence, arms or cloathing, which are due to them by the Continent. It is an extraordinary bounty intended to render the condition of the Soldier more pleasant, and not to hold place of the things which they ought to receive from the Congress, or from the States.

10th. If the General judges necessary, he will publish at the end of a certain time, an amount of that which shall have been received from each particular State.

11th. The Women who shall send their offerings, will have in their choice to conceal or to give their names; and if it shall be thought proper, on a fit occasion, to publish one day the lists, they only, who shall consent, shall be named; when with regard to the sums sent, there will be no mention made, if they so desire it.

PRINTED BY JOHN DUNLAP.

175. Verso of *The Sentiments of an American Woman*

A POEM,

Spoken Extempore, by a YOUNG LADY, on hearing the Guns firing and Bells chiming on account of the great and Glorious Acquisition of their Excellencies Gen. WASHINGTON and the C. de GRASSE, by the Surrender of *York-Town*, in which were Ld. *Cornwallis* and Army, confisting of Nine Thousand Troops, a Forty Gun Ship, a Frigate, an armed Veffel and One Hundred Sail of Tranfports.

HONOR commands great WASHINGTON I fing,
The noble feat of Count de GRASSE muft ring,
Who has *Cornwallis* now within his power,
With all his Army in an evil hour.
Brave GREENE I fing, with all the Patriot Sons,
But moft adore Great Godlike WASHINGTON ;
YORK-TOWN once more is freed from Britifh chains,
Rejoice AMERICA now FREEDOM reigns :
FREEDOM is Our's ; vain Britons boaft no more
Thy matchlefs ftrength by fea, nor on the fhore,
Great WASHINGTON doth thunder thro' the plain,
And piles the field with mountains of the flain ;
His foes they tremble and his name adore,
Confefs his might 'till time fhall be no more ;
Brave Count de GRASSE ! Nine thoufand men did fall
Into the hands of this brave Admiral ;
Captur'd by him, how wondrous 'tis to tell,
Befides a frigate and an arm'd veffel.
A fhip of forty guns then met the fate
Of cruel war, and own this Hero great ;
hundred fail of tranfports then did yield,
confefs him brave by fea as in the field.
Let the brave VICTORS on their conqueft fmile,
And fafe enjoy the triumph of their toil.
Let FREEDOM's DAUGHTERS weave a garland white
Of pureft Lillies with fupreme delight ;
Thro'out the world may it be ever faid,
They plac'd this chaplet on their Heroes HEAD.

Printed by E. RUSSELL, near Liberty-Stump.--At the fame Place may be had, RUSSELL'S AMERICAN ALMANAC, and BICKERSTAFF'S BOSTON do.

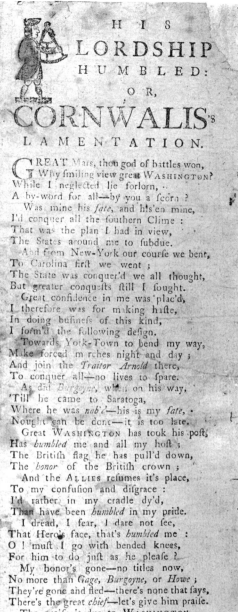

HIS LORDSHIP HUMBLED: OR, CORNWALIS's LAMENTATION.

GREAT Mars, thou god of battles won,
Why fmiling view great WASHINGTON?
While I neglected lie forlorn,
A by-word for all—by you a fcorn ?
Was mine his *fate*, and his'en mine,
I'd conquer all the fouthern Clime :
That was the plan I had in view,
The States around me to fubdue.
And from New-York our courfe we bent,
To Carolina firft we went ;
The State was conquer'd we all thought,
But greater conquefts ftill I fought.
Great confidence in me was plac'd,
I therefore was for making hafte,
In doing bufinefs of this kind,
I form'd the following defign.
Towards York-Town to bend my way,
Make forced marches night and day ;
And join the *Traitor Arnold* there,
To conquer all—no lives to fpare.
As did *Burgoyne*, when on his way,
'Till he came to Saratoga,
Where he was *nab'd*—his is my *fate*,
Nought can be done—it is too late.
Great WASHINGTON has took his poft,
Has *humbled* me and all my hoft ;
The Britifh flag he has pull'd down,
The *honor* of the Britifh crown ;
And the ALLIES refumes it's place,
To my confufion and difgrace :
I'd rather in my cradle dy'd,
Than have been *humbled* in my pride.
I dread, I fear, I dare not fee,
That Hero's face, that's *humbled* me :
O ! muft I go with bended knees,
For him to do juft as he pleafe ?
My honor's gone—no titles now,
No more than *Gage*, *Burgoyne*, or *Howe* ;
They're gone and fled—there's none that fays,
There's the great *chief*—let's give him praife.
The praife is due to WASHINGTON,
Whofe *glory now, and ever fhone* :
See that great CHIEF, triumphant ftands,
Smiles at my lofs—defies my bands.
It pierces me—I feel the fmart,
Juft like a dagger to my heart ;
To think I brag'd and made fuch boafts,
What I'd do 'mongft rebel hofts.
That with my Britifh German bands,
Would fpread the *terrors* of my hands,
And crufh rebellion from this fhore,
Ne'er to be heard amongft them more.
My brags are now come to an *end*,
I wifh to find fome *honeft* friend,
That would affift me in my trouble,
And help me out of this bad *hobble.*

180. A poem celebrating Cornwallis's defeat at Yorktown

The two poems printed on this broadside both celebrate the defeat of Cornwallis at Yorktown. The one on the left, written by a young woman, sings the praises of Washington and the French commander, Count de Grasse, and rejoices over the victory of freedom. The poem on the right has been attributed to Cornwallis himself, and it laments the British defeats, but praises 'Great Washington.' The woodcut of Washington on the left shows him facing Liberty as Fame blows his horn to signal the American triumph.

181

Mrs. General Washington, Bestowing Thirteen Stripes on Britannia

Engraving, [London], 1783. British Museum Catalogue 6202.

Published in the *Rambler's Magazine*, this engraving shows Washington brandishing a scourge as Britannia tries to escape. Representatives of France, Spain, and Holland encourage Washington, who summarizes the lesson of the American colonial experience: 'Parents should not behave like Tyrants to their Children.'

182

. . . The Definitive Treaty, Between Great-Britain and the United States of America, Signed at Paris the 3rd Day of September, 1783

Baltimore, [1783]. Evans 18252.

After the defeat of Cornwallis, the British suffered further setbacks at the hands of the French in the West Indies in 1781 and early 1782. Consequently, Britain's desire for peace was enhanced, and in March 1782 Lord North resigned. He was replaced by Lord Rockingham, the minister who had secured the repeal of the Stamp Act in 1766. The new ministry immediately opened direct negotiations with the American peace commissioners.

This is the Treaty which officially ended the hostilities between the United States and Britain in January 1783. The British recognized American independence and also ceded to the new nation territory stretching from the Atlantic to the Mississippi and from the Canadian border to Florida.

183

The United States of America Laid Down from the Best Authorities Agreeable to the Peace of 1783

London, 1783.

This beautifully rendered map illustrates the United States of America at the time of the Treaty of Paris of 1783. The area bordered in green, stretching to the Mississippi River on the west, Florida on the south, and Canada on the north, seemed to demonstrate the partial fulfillment of America's destiny, for now the country was spreading out to fill the continent. The elegant cartouche shows George Washington next to Liberty. Fame trumpets a salute to the American flag with thirteen stars. To the right Benjamin Franklin, who helped negotiate the terms of peace, is taking dictation from Justice (with the blindfold) and Minerva, the goddess of wisdom.

Fruits of the Revolution

With independence most of the states drafted new constitutions. Most Americans, however, feared the executive power that the king and his ministers had exercised during the years of imperial crisis. Thus they formulated republican constitutions with most of the power lodged in the lower houses of legislatures. The Articles of Confederation similarly placed national powers in the Congress.

These new state and national governments were significant because they were the first efforts in the modern western world to define and set forth in writing the means by which governmental power was to be exercised. Though the state constitutions proved to be successful, the Articles of Confederation had many weaknesses and inadequacies, and by the mid-1780s many political leaders began to consider the creation of a stronger central government.

184

The Constitution of the State of New-York

Fish-Kill, New York, 1777. Evans 15472.

New York and Maryland were the only states whose constitutions gave independent powers to an upper legislative chamber. In New York the senate was endowed with a considerable measure of executive power as well as legislative power equal to that of the lower house. New York also differed from the other states by giving the governor a three-year term, a legislative veto, and power to make a wide range of administrative appointments. Elsewhere, however, the upper house and the governor were thoroughly dependent upon, or subordinate to, the lower house.

185

A Bill for Establishing the Constitution, of the State of South-Carolina

Charleston, 1777. Evans 20716.

This pamphlet contains the text of the proposed state constitution for South Carolina. Adopted in 1777, the South Carolina constitution, like many other new state constitutions, placed most of the power in the lower house of the legislature. The printing of the document made the particulars of the framework of government—as well as the rights and liberties of the people—available for all to read. Early editions of the state constitutions are uncommon. This pamphlet is one of two recorded copies.

186

A Declaration of Rights, and Plan of Government for the State of New-Hampshire

Exeter, 1779. Evans 16386.

This Declaration of Rights spells out in simple language the reasons why the citizens of New Hampshire were engaged in the Revolution. The Plan of Government also states in easily understood terms the nature of the republic that the delegates of New Hampshire were creating.

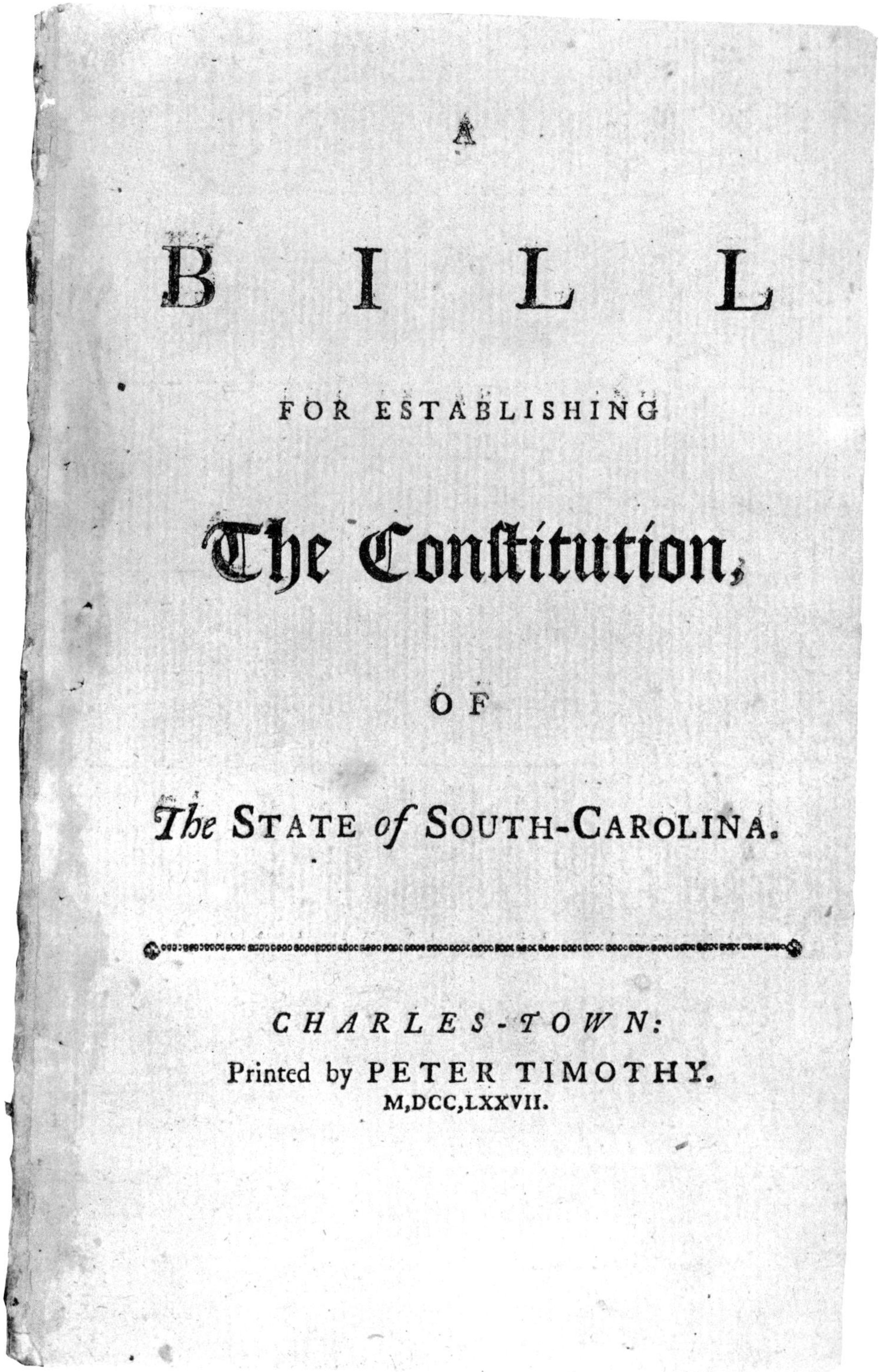

A

BILL

FOR ESTABLISHING

The Constitution,

OF

The STATE of SOUTH-CAROLINA.

⬥⬥

CHARLES-TOWN:
Printed by PETER TIMOTHY.
M,DCC,LXXVII.

185. The proposed state constitution of South Carolina

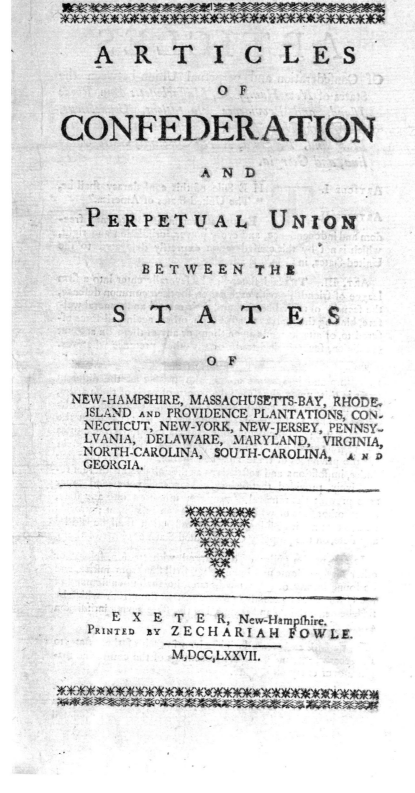

ARTICLES

OF

CONFEDERATION

AND

PERPETUAL UNION

BETWEEN THE

STATES

OF

NEW-HAMPSHIRE, MASSACHUSETTS-BAY, RHODE-ISLAND AND PROVIDENCE PLANTATIONS, CONNECTICUT, NEW-YORK, NEW-JERSEY, PENNSYLVANIA, DELAWARE, MARYLAND, VIRGINIA, NORTH-CAROLINA, SOUTH-CAROLINA, AND GEORGIA.

EXETER, New-Hampfhire.
PRINTED BY ZECHARIAH FOWLE.

M,DCC,LXXVII.

187. The Articles of Confederation

187

Articles of Confederation and Perpetual Union

Exeter, New Hampshire, 1777. Evans 15624. Gift of Donald M. Frost, 1941.

The Articles of Confederation provided a loose form of government for the thirteen rebelling colonies. John Dickinson drafted the plan which provided for a permanent single-branch national government, consisting only of a congress organized much like the Continental Congress. The Articles were adopted November 15, 1777, and went into effect March 1, 1781. They remained the frame of government for the union until the government under the Constitution went into effect in 1789.

188

An Ordinance for the Government of the Territory of the United States, North-West of the River Ohio

[New York, 1787.] Evans 20779. Gift of the Massachusetts Historical Society, 1962, honoring the sesquicentennial anniversary of AAS.

One of the greatest accomplishments of the United States under the Articles of Confederation was the Northwest Ordinance. It established the machinery for the settlement and eventual statehood of the territories northwest of the Ohio River, on an equal basis with states already established. The orderly expansion of a 'great republican empire' was thereby made possible.

189   JOHN JAY (1745–1829)

Circular, January 29, 1785

Manuscript, John Jay Papers.

Jay's task as secretary for the Department of Foreign Affairs under the Articles of Confederation was severely hampered by the decentralized nature of that government. In this letter addressed to the governor of Connecticut, for example, Jay requested a copy of the laws of the state and information on internal affairs so that he could conduct foreign negotiations without violating any of that state's laws or interests. Similar letters were also sent to the other governors. While these correspondences were courteous gestures on Jay's part, they also demonstrated the fact that the real power, or sovereignty, in 1785 resided in each individual state and not in the United States as a whole.

190   ROGER SHERMAN (1721–1793)

Remarks on a Pamphlet . . .

[New Haven], 1784. Evans 18782.

Sherman was a member of the Continental Congress from Connecticut and an author of the Articles of Confederation. He later proposed a series of amendments designed to strengthen the Confederation. As this pamphlet indicates, problems concerning western lands were of special interest to him. He knew that only a strong national government could properly govern, and preserve for future growth, the great expanse of territory in the American West. Thus in 1787, he became convinced of the need for a new constitution.

The signing of the peace treaty in 1783 signalled the beginning of two years of prosperity, but in 1785-1786 an acute economic depression swept over the nation. Imports and exports dropped steadily from their 1785 levels and farm wages fell twenty per cent. Moreover money shortages increased drastically, creditors became more insistent on prompt payment of debts, and high taxes became higher. In the winter of 1786–1787, roving bands of debtors and impoverished farmers, fed up with their economic plight and led by a Revolutionary veteran and farmer named Daniel Shays, seized control of the interior of Massachusetts.

Shays led an army of almost two thousand men, but in February 1787 the state militia, under the command of Benjamin Lincoln, routed his force. Shays remained convinced that he had been fighting for the same principle he had fought for in the Revolution: freedom from economic oppression. Most of the rest of the country, however, believed Shays's Rebellion a sign that a strong national government was needed to prevent 'the rabble' from subverting peace, order, and security.

191

To the Honourable Senate and the Honourable House of Representatives in General Court Assembled the Petition of the Convention in the County of Worcester

Manuscript, September 28, 1786. Shays's Rebellion Collection.

Daniel Shays headed the committee of indebted farmers who presented petitions and resolutions such as this one to various Common Pleas and General Sessions Courts in Massachusetts. The farmers sought relief from the acute economic depression of the mid-1780s which made it extremely difficult for individuals to pay their debts or taxes. The petitions demanded that courts refrain from hearing such cases, and when their pleas were ignored, the farmers closed several courts. The protest then became an armed insurrection.

192

Commonwealth of Massachusetts, By Benjamin Lincoln, Esquire . . .

No place, [1787]. Unrecorded. Given in memory of Daniel W. Lincoln, 1971.

Benjamin Lincoln (1733–1810) was chosen by the Massachusetts legislature to suppress Shays's Rebellion. After doing so, Lincoln offered pardons to Shays and his followers if they would lay down their arms and swear allegiance to the Commonwealth of Massachusetts. Most of the insurgents responded positively to Lincoln's offer. Shays himself requested and received a pardon one year later.

193

An Address from the General Court to the People of the Commonwealth of Massachusetts

Boston, 1786. Evans 19781.

This pamphlet was issued by the Massachusetts legislature, or General Court, in an attempt to counter some of the effects of Shays's Rebellion. Members of the legislature feared that the insurrection might become uncontrollable should it spread to the eastern part of the state. To avoid this, the Court emphasized what measures the state had taken to relieve the economic burdens of farmers and debtors, and repeatedly warned about the dangers of a breakdown of law and order.

Commonwealth of MASSACHUSETTS,

By BENJAMIN LINCOLN, ESQUIRE,

Commanding General of the Troops now in the Field, by Order of GOVERNMENT.

WHEREAS there are some of the Citizens of this Commonwealth, who have acted in Arms as Non-Commissioned Officers and Privates against the Government of this State, who have caused it to be represented, that they would willingly return to their Allegiance and Duty, could they hope for a Pardon.

To all such I declare, That if they will come in, surrender their Arms, and take and subscribe the Oath of Allegiance to this Commonwealth, that they will be recommended to a Pardon.

B. LINCOLN.

Dated at Head-Quarters, Pittsfield, *February* 19, 1787.

192. The pardon offered by Gen. Benjamin Lincoln to those men involved in Shays's Rebellion

194 ISAAC BACKUS (1724–1806)

An Address to the Inhabitants of New-England, Concerning the Present Bloody Controversy Therein

Boston, 1787. Evans 20212.

Backus was a Baptist minister, historian, and champion of religious liberty, whose fame rests in his protest against civil control of religion. An earnest lover of liberty, he also recognized the importance of order and law. Thus, after Shays's Rebellion in 1786, he became concerned that America's special mission was in grave peril. In this address he pointed out that though the founding fathers had come to America 'for purity and liberty,' the current upheaval in Massachusetts had caused a dark cloud to descend upon the country.

195 GEORGE RICHARDS MINOT (1758–1802)

The History of the Insurrections, in Massachusetts

Worcester, 1788. Evans 21259.

Minot was a jurist and historian who made his mark by writing this history of Shays's Rebellion. The account, which was not sympathetic to the rebels' cause, stressed the need for a strong government to suppress disorder. Minot subsequently wrote a history of Massachusetts.

THE FEDERAL CONSTITUTION

By 1786 several weaknesses of the Articles of Confederation had become obvious. Financial problems, the weak image of the United States abroad, and the fact of domestic disorder as evidenced by Shays's Rebellion particularly caused much alarm. Accordingly, Congress appointed a committee to revise the Articles but the recommendations were tabled because of the impossibility of obtaining unanimous approval from the states. Meanwhile, in September 1786, delegates from several states met at Annapolis to discuss interstate commerce problems, and decided to reconvene at Philadelphia in May 1787 to revise the Articles. The result of this new convention was the Constitution.

The Constitution of the United States created the federal system by which sovereignty was shared by the national and state governments and under which foreign, financial, and domestic problems could be resolved more efficiently by the national government. Before the new Constitution could take effect, however, it had to be ratified by at least nine of the thirteen states. Despite strong opposition from those who wished to retain the Articles, the new system was ratified by eleven states in less than a year. The first presidential election took place early in 1789 and the first Congress convened in New York shortly thereafter.

196

The Constitution of the United States of America

State Gazette of South Carolina, Charleston, October 4, 1787.

This is one of the first newspaper printings of the new Constitution. Printed in its entirety, it is accompanied by the resolutions of the convention, dated September 17, 1787, concerning the procedure for ratification. Also printed, following the resolutions, is George Washington's explanation of the need for a new constitution and his request that this one be adopted.

197

The Constitution or Frame of Government, for the United States of America

Boston, 1787. Evans 20801.

This is the first pamphlet printing of the new Constitution. The General Court of the Commonwealth of Massachusetts ordered it printed so that the people of the state could have a better understanding of the new government. Most of the other states soon followed the lead of Massachusetts and reprinted the Constitution.

retain the blank leaves

THE
CONSTITUTION
OR FRAME OF
GOVERNMENT,
FOR THE
UNITED STATES
OF
AMERICA,

As reported by the CONVENTION of DELEGATES, from the UNITED STATES, begun and held at *PHILADEL-PHIA*, on the firſt *Monday* of *May*, 1787, and continued by Adjournments to the ſeventeenth Day of *September* following.—Which they reſolved, ſhould be laid before the *United States* in Congreſs Aſſembled ; and afterwards be ſubmitted to a Convention of Delegates, choſen in each State, by the *People* thereof, under the recommendation of its Legiſlature, for their *Aſſent* and *Ratification.*

TOGETHER with the reſolutions of the *General Court* of the *Commonwealth* of *Maſſachuſetts*, for calling ſaid *Convention*, agreeable to the recommendation of CONGRESS.

Publiſhed by Order of Government.

PRINTED at BOSTON, MASSACHUSETTS,
BY ADAMS and NOURSE,
Printers to the Honourable the GENERAL COURT.
M,DCC,LXXXVII.

1787

197. The first pamphlet printing of the Constitution

198 RICHARD HENRY LEE (1733–1794)

Observations Leading to a Fair Examination of the System of Government Proposed by the Late Convention

[New York?, 1787.] Evans 20454.

Lee was a member of the Virginia House of Burgesses and an active participant in the American Revolution. On June 7, 1776, he proposed a declaration of independence. Later, he was a strong supporter of the Articles of Confederation, though he knew that they were defective. Subsequently Lee led the opposition to the Constitution, and in a series of 'Letters of the Federal Farmer,' he laid down the Antifederalist dogma. This pamphlet examined the 'flaws' in the proposed new government and suggested several remedies. One of these was a bill of rights, for which he vigorously fought when he became one of the first two United States senators from Virginia.

199

The Federalist: A Collection of Essays, Written in Favour of the New Constitution

2 vols. in one, New York, 1788. Evans 21127. Gift of Alfred L. Aiken, 1941.

Written by Alexander Hamilton, John Jay, and James Madison, the essays in *The Federalist* were originally published in several New York newspapers to persuade the American people to ratify the new Constitution. The collection is generally regarded as the most important contribution to political science made in our country. *The Federalist* Number Ten, written by James Madison, argued that the main problem of government was to reconcile the rivalries among the various economic groups which compose society. He argued that the form of government provided in the proposed Constitution (republicanism) was more likely than any other to hold an even balance among these groups and to prevent any one interest from unduly exploiting its rivals.

200 JOHN JAY (1745–1829)

An Address to the People of the State of New-York on the Subject of the Constitution

New York, [1788]. Evans 21175.

Jay was a statesman and diplomat who negotiated the controversial treaty with Great Britain known as Jay's Treaty (1794). Previously he had helped write *The Federalist* with James Madison and Alexander Hamilton. During the ratification controversy he penned several pamphlets, including this one, in an attempt to persuade reluctant New Yorkers to accept the new government.

201

Federal Song, On the Adoption of the Federal Constitution, by the State of New-Hampshire, June 21st, 1788

No place, [1788]. Unrecorded.

This patriotic song celebrated the themes of union, freedom, and peace. It is typical of many such poems and songs written by Federalists to support the new government.

202

State of Rhode Island and Providence Plantations. In General Assembly. January Session, A.D. 1790. An Act for Calling a Convention to Take into Consideration the Constitution Proposed for the United States

[Providence, 1790.] Evans 22840.

This broadside calls for a convention to consider the Federal Constitution. The Rhode Island convention would be 'fully authorized, finally to decide on the said Constitution,' and thus determine whether or not the state would become part of the new government.

FEDERAL SONG,
On the adoption of the
FEDERAL CONSTITUTION,
by the State of
NEW-HAMPSHIRE,
June 21st, 1788.
[To be sung at the Celebration, the 26th.]

To the Tune,—*He comes, he comes.*

I.
IT comes ! it comes ! high raise the song
The bright procession moves along.
From pole to pole refound the NINE,
And diftant worlds the chorus join.

II.
In vain did Britain forge the chain,
While countlefs fquadrons hid the plain,
HANTONIA, foremoft of the NINE,
Defy'd their force, and took Burgoyne.

To the tune,—"*Smile, fmile, Britannia.*"

III.
When PEACE refum'd her feat,
And Freedom *feem'd* fecure,
Our patriot-fages met,
That Freedom to infure :
Then ev'ry eye on us was turn'd,
And ev'ry breaft indignant burn'd.

IV.
That haughty race (they faid)
All government defpife ;
Skill'd in the martial trade,
More valiant far than wife.
Though PALLAS leads them to the field,
Her aid in council is withheld.

V.
Falfe charge ! (the Goddefs cry'd)
I made each hardy fon
Who in war's purple tide
Firft laid the *Corner-Stone*,
His utmoft energy employ
To bring the TOP-STONE forth with joy.

To the firft tune,—"*He comes,*" &c.

VI.
Tis done ! the glorious fabric's rear'd !
Still be New-Hampshire's fons rever'd.
Who fix'd its BASE in blood and fcars,
And ftretch'd its TURRETS to the ftars !

To the tune,—"*When Britons firft,*" &c.

VII.
See each induftrious ART moves on
To afk protection, praife, and fame ;
The PLOUGHMAN by his tools is known,
And VULCAN, NEPTUNE, join their claim ;
Allow them all ; and wifely prove
Nought can exift long without LOVE.

VIII.
LOVE binds in peace the univerfe ;
By LOVE focieties combine ;
LOVE prompts the Poet's rapt'rous verfe,
And makes thefe humble lays divine :
Then fhout for UNION, heav'n-born dame !
And crown the goblet to her name.

To the firft Tune.

IX.
May HAMPSHIRE's fons in peace and war,
Supremely great ! both laurels wear,
Still from her neighbours bear the prize,
Till the laft blaze involves the fkies !

201. A song celebrating the ratification of the Constitution by New Hampshire

In 1788, Rhode Island had held a popular referendum on the question which soundly voted down the Constitution. The Convention called for in this act ratified the Constitution on May 29, 1790, making Rhode Island the last of the thirteen original states to do so.

203

Amendments Proposed to be Added to the Federal Constitution by the Congress of the United States of America

Boston, 1790. Evans 22953.

These amendments, which quickly became known as the Bill of Rights, were added to the Constitution in order to secure the continued support of several states. Massachusetts, for example, had ratified the Constitution with the recommendation that such a bill of rights be added. When Congress agreed to these amendments several other reluctant states also ratified, and the new government became operative.

204   JOHN WOODHULL (1744–1824)

A Sermon for the Day of Publick Thanksgiving

Trenton, New Jersey, 1790. Evans 23089.

A clergyman and ardent patriot, Woodhull had managed to persuade every male member of his congregation capable of bearing arms to fight in the Revolution to preserve American liberty. This sermon, delivered in 1789, contains Woodhull's views on the future glory of the United States. He believed that the new Constitution had been created with God's guidance in order to secure America's destiny.

WASHINGTON AND THE NEW GOVERNMENT

The nation was fortunate to have George Washington as its first president. He gave the presidency the dignity, strength, and legitimacy that only his personality could provide.

One of Washington's most important appointments was Alexander Hamilton as secretary of the treasury. Hamilton's administrative genius and fiscal policies welded the nation together with bonds of economic interest which benefited all segments of society.

Other problems faced by the new government were resolved by Congress, in spite of the emergence of two distinct political parties revolving around the leadership of Hamilton and Jefferson. European turmoils after 1793 promoted party conflict, and by the end of Washington's second term the Federalists and Republicans openly vied for national leadership. Nevertheless, Washington's presidency had served the United States well, and when he died in 1799 the bereaved nation deified its first hero.

205

Congress of the United States: At the Third Session, Begun and Held at the City of Philadelphia on Monday the Sixth of December, One Thousand Seven Hundred and Ninety

[Philadelphia, 1791.] Evans 23878.

This act supplemented Alexander Hamilton's bank bill, and, like his funding and assumption schemes, was designed to link personal economic interests to the strength and well-being of the country. Hamilton's programs provided the basic economic machinery for the growth and future strength of the United States.

206 FISHER AMES (1758-1808)

The Original Manuscript Copy of a Sketch of the Character of Alexander Hamilton, 1804

Manuscript.

This eulogy on Alexander Hamilton, who died in 1804, was written by the arch-Federalist Fisher Ames. With Hamilton, Ames believed that the federal government was weak. Thus it had to reach out for power, acquire popular prestige by a vigorous, energetic policy, and depend on an aristocracy of talent and virtue. He believed that Hamilton was a perfect example of someone with the kind of virtue and ability necessary for leadership, and he greatly lamented his death. In this manuscript, Ames recounted Hamilton's life and discussed his great contributions to the financial and political stability of the country. Ames closed by stating that the continued prosperity of America would depend on its ability to learn from Hamilton's example.

207

Plan of the City of Washington in the Territory of Columbia

Philadelphia, 1792. Wheat and Brun 531.

The plan of the national capitol was surveyed by Andrew Ellicott and was designed by Pierre Charles L'Enfant, a Frenchman who had fought in the Revolution. The design is not without grandeur. L'Enfant demonstrated subtlety and skill by imposing a gridiron on the radial avenues beloved by the French. Moreover, it is to L'Enfant that we owe the vista of the Capitol from The Mall, and that of the White House from the Potomac.

208

Proclamation. By the President of the United States

[Boston, 1793.] Evans 26336.

116

In February 1793 France declared war on England. Hoping to avoid American involvement in that conflict, President Washington issued this famous proclamation of neutrality on April 22, 1793. He asserted that the United States was disposed to 'pursue a conduct friendly and impartial towards the Belligerent powers.' He warned American citizens 'to avoid all acts and proceedings whatsoever, which may in any manner tend to contravene such disposition.' Though Washington avoided war, this proclamation added impetus to a growing split between the Republicans, who favored France, and the Federalists, who favored England.

209

Treaty with Great Britain, Mercury Office, Saturday, July 4

[Boston, 1795.] Bristol 8977. MP 47307.

This treaty with Great Britain was negotiated by John Jay, by whose name it is generally known. Among the twenty-eight articles are provisions for the evacuation of those Northwest Territory posts still occupied by the British, the setting up of arbitration machinery for the settlement of disputed boundaries and private debts, and the opening of limited American trade in the British East and West Indies. When the terms of the treaty became known in March 1795, however, Jay was condemned in petitions and newspaper articles and was hanged in effigy in various towns and cities. All this helped broaden the growing gap between the Federalists, who favored the treaty, and the Republicans, who condemned it. The Federalists prevailed, for the treaty was ratified by the Senate in June 1795.

210 GEORGE WASHINGTON (1732-1799)

. . . By the President of the United States of America, a Proclamation

[Philadelphia, 1795.] Evans 29730.

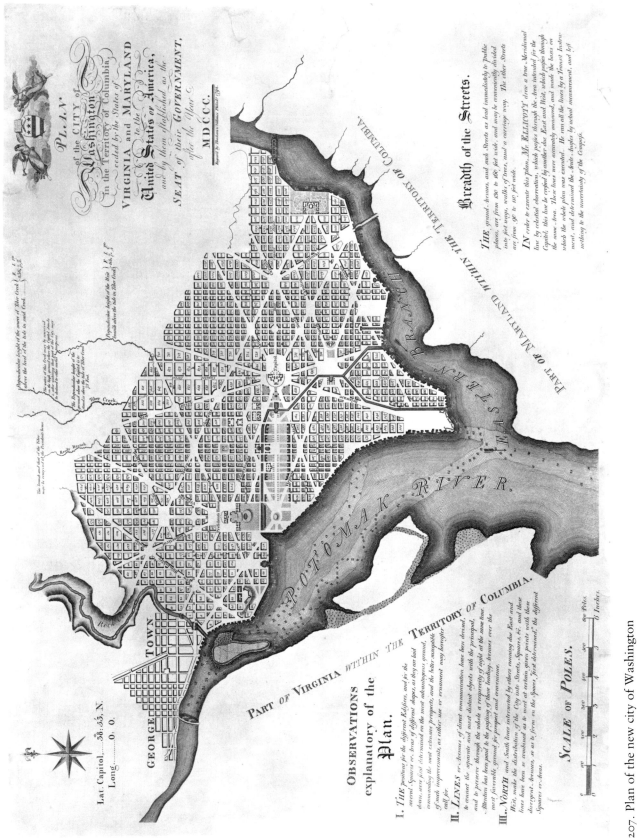

PLAN
of the CITY of
Washington
in the Territory of Columbia,
ceded by the States of
VIRGINIA and **MARYLAND** to the
United States of **America,**
and by them established as the
SEAT of their **GOVERNMENT,**
after the Year
__MDCCC.__

Engraved by Thackara & Vallance Philad. 1792.

Lat. Capitol......38. 53. N.
Long............ 0. 0.

GEORGE
TOWN

Rock

Tiber Creek

Reedy Branch

The Ground Plan of the Tiber may be conveyed to the carry of the Presidents house.

Perpendicular height of the source of Tiber Creek { F. I.ns above the level of the tide in said Creek } 236. 7,2

Perpendicular height of the Wells { F. Ins above the tide in Tiber Creek } 116. 7,2

In notion of this Creek may be conveyed to the high ground where the Capitol stands, above the level of the City may be situated so many sources, proportional.

The Perpendicular height of the ground where the Capitol is to stands above the tide in Tiber Creek 78 Feet.

PART OF MARYLAND WITHIN THE TERRITORY OF COLUMBIA

EASTERN BRANCH

POTOMAK RIVER

PART OF VIRGINIA WITHIN THE TERRITORY OF COLUMBIA.

Breadth of the Streets.

THE grand avenues, and such Streets as lead immediately to public places, are from 130 to 160 feet wide; and may be conveniently divided into foot ways, walks of trees, and a carriage way. The other Streets are from 90 to 110 feet wide.

IN order to execute this plan, Mr. ELLICOTT drew a true Meridional line by celestial observation, which passes through the Area intended for the Capitol: this line he crossed by another due East and West, which passes through the same Area. These lines were accurately measured, and made the bases on which the whole plan was executed. He ran all the lines by a Transit Instrument, and determined the Acute Angles by actual measurement, and left nothing to the uncertainty of the Compass.

OBSERVATIONS
explanatory of the
Plan.

I. THE positions for the different Edifices, and for the several Squares or Areas of different shapes, as they are laid down, were first determined on the most advantageous ground, commanding the most extensive prospects, and the better-susceptible of such improvements as either use or ornament may hereafter call for.

II. LINES or Avenues of direct communication have been devised, to connect the separate and most distant objects with the principal, and to preserve through the whole a reciprocity of sight at the same time. Attention has been paid to the passing of these leading Avenues over the most favorable ground for prospect and convenience.

III. NORTH and South lines intersected by others running due East and West, make the distribution of the City into Streets, Squares, &c. and these lines have been so combined as to meet at certain given points with those divergent Avenues, so as to form on the Spaces "first determined," the different Squares or Areas.

SCALE OF POLES.

By The President
OF THE UNITED STATES OF AMERICA,
A Proclamation.

WHEN we review the calamities which afflict so many other Nations, the present condition of the *United States* affords much matter of consolation and satisfaction. Our exemption hitherto from foreign war----an increasing prospect of the continuance of that exemption----the great degree of internal tranquillity we have enjoyed----the recent confirmation of that tranquillity, by the suppression of an insurrection which so wantonly threatened it----the happy course of our public affairs in general----the unexampled prosperity of all classes of our Citizens, are circumstances which peculiarly mark our situation with indications of the Divine Benificence towards us. In such a state of things it is, in an especial manner, our duty as a People, with devout reverence and affectionate gratitude, to acknowledge our many and great obligations to ALMIGHTY GOD, and to implore him to continue and confirm the blessings we experience.

Deeply penetrated with this sentiment, I GEORGE WASHINGTON, President of the United States, do recommend to all Religious Societies and Denominations, and to all Persons whomsoever within the United States, to set apart and observe *THURSDAY* the *Nineteenth* day of *February* next, as a Day of PUBLIC THANKSGIVING and PRAYER ; and on that Day to meet together, and render their sincere and hearty thanks to the Great Ruler of Nations, for the manifold and signal mercies, which distinguish our lot as a nation ; particularly for the possession of Constitutions of Government, which unite, and by their union establish liberty with order----for the preservation of our Peace foreign and domestic----for the seasonable controul which has been given to a spirit of disorder, in the suppression of the late Insurrection----and generally, for the prosperous course of our affairs public and private ; and at the same time, humbly and fervently to beseech the Kind Author of these Blessings, graciously to prolong them to us----to imprint on our hearts a deep and solemn sense of our obligations to Him for them----to teach us rightly to estimate their immense value----to preserve us from the arrogance of prosperity, and from hazarding the advantages we enjoy by delusive pursuits---to dispose us to merit the continuance of his favours, by not abusing them, by our gratitude for them, and by a correspondent conduct as Citizens and as Men---to render this Country more and more a safe and propitious Asylum for the unfortunate of other Countries ---to extend among us true and useful knowledge---to diffuse and establish habits of sobriety, order, morality and piety ; and finally, to impart all the blessings we possess, or ask for ourselves, to the whole Family of Mankind.

 In Testimony Whereof, I have caused the SEAL of the UNITED STATES of AMERICA to be affixed to these Presents, and signed the same with my Hand. Done at the city of PHILADELPHIA, the first day of *January,* one thousand seven hundred and ninety-five, and of the Independence of the United States of America the nineteenth.

G°: WASHINGTON.

By The President---EDM: RANDOLPH.

210. Thanksgiving proclamation issued by President Washington

This proclamation by the First President reveals his (and most Americans') attitudes about the nation, its role in the world, its good fortune, and its destiny. Washington proclaimed that a day of public thanksgiving be celebrated on February 19, 1796, so that Americans could thank God for the peace, wealth, liberty, and order with which they had been blessed, and to implore God for the continuation of those blessings.

211 GEORGE WASHINGTON (1732–1799)

To the People of the United States

Newport, [1796]. Evans 31539.

This is one of many contemporary editions of President Washington's 'Farewell Address.' Printed in Newport, Rhode Island, it was distributed in the town as a handbill. In it Washington spoke of America's past triumphs, her contemporary problems, and her great future. He urged that party alliances be avoided at all costs. He also cautioned his successors to remain free of 'dangerous foreign entanglements' which could involve the nation in needless wars and sap it of its economic strength. He concluded that Americans had to be ever vigilant against threats to

their liberties and that they must remain virtuous and godly or else they would not fulfill their destiny.

212 ISAAC BALL

Inscribed to the Memory of the American Fabius, by Doctor Isaac Ball, of New York

[New York, 1800.] Evans 36880.

This memorial to George Washington, who died December 14, 1799, was written by a New York physician and surgeon. A towering legend even before he died, Washington's fame, reputation, and deeds would gain him almost divine proportions after his death.

213 THOMAS CLARKE

Sacred to the Memory of the Illustrious G. Washington

Engraving, Boston, 1801. Stauffer 408.

Three allegorical figures express their sorrow over the passing of George Washington, whose face is clearly visible on a tomb engraved with the inscription 'There is rest in Heaven.' Portraits and memorials such as this proliferated after Washington died, and helped transform the man into legend.

THE PRESIDENCY OF JOHN ADAMS

Throughout the early 1790s the Federalists and Republicans had competed for political power. With Washington retiring in 1796 they vied for the presidency. After a bitter campaign, John Adams was elected president by a narrow margin over Thomas Jefferson, who became vice-president. In 1797 President Adams appointed a commission to seek a treaty of commerce and amity with France. In Paris the commissioners were visited by three agents—known in the American dis-

patches only as 'X,' 'Y,' and 'Z'—of French Foreign Minister Talleyrand. They indicated to the Americans that, unless a bribe was offered Talleyrand and a loan provided for France, war would result.

In 1798 strong pro-French and anti-British protests forced Adams to submit the XYZ correspondence to Congress. Public opinion immediately turned against France, and the country prepared for war. Washington was called from retirement to serve as commander-in-chief, the Navy Department was established, and existing treaties with France were nullified. Two years of undeclared war with France followed. Feeling threatened by enemies from both within and without, the Federalist-controlled Congress passed the Alien and Sedition Acts. These laws outraged the Republicans who passed the Virginia and Kentucky Resolutions to protest such unconstitutional assaults on civil liberties and the prerogatives of the states.

Adams managed to resolve most of these tensions and avoid a declared war with France. But he split his own party in the process. As a result, the election of 1800 brought about the triumph of Jeffersonian Republicanism known as the Revolution of 1800.

214 ABIGAIL ADAMS (1744–1818)

Letter, May 24, 1797

Manuscript. Abigail Adams Letters.

Abigail Adams, the wife of the second president, was an ardent Federalist and quite capable of tart comments on political topics and personalities. In this letter, written to her sister Mary Cranch, she discussed the 'vile and debauched' condition of Washington, D.C., then under construction, and lamented the flourishing speculation 'in Property, in politicks and in Religion.' This is only one of hundreds of letters in a similar vein written by a perceptive and articulate woman who has been called the greatest letter writer America has ever produced.

215

The Alien and Sedition Laws, and Virginia and Kentucky Resolutions

[Boston, 1798.] Evans 34711.

Congress prepared for war with France in 1798 by passing a series of measures designed to suppress disloyalty at home. Known collectively as the Alien and Sedition Acts, they discriminated harshly against aliens and severely curtailed freedom of speech and press. These laws were anathema to Republicans who responded with the Kentucky and Virginia Resolutions. These state resolves declared that the Alien and Sedition Acts were unconstitutional and that whenever the federal government violated the Constitution it was the right and duty of the states to nullify such acts. Neither Virginia nor Kentucky took any concrete steps to nullify the laws, however.

216 JOHN ADAMS (1735–1826)

Message from the President of the United States

Philadelphia, 1799. Evans 36547.

When Messrs. X, Y, and Z informed the United States Commissioners in Paris that negotiations for a treaty with France could begin only after a bribe and a loan, the Americans refused with righteous indignation. After President Adams saw reports of the XYZ affair, he considered asking for a declaration of war. Congress demanded to see the reports and Adams delivered them in this address of January 21, 1799. Both houses were outraged and when this 'Message' was published the public clamored for war. Mr. W, referred to in the text, was Nicholas Hubbard, an employee of a Dutch banking house, but his participation was minimal.

217 ROBERT TREAT PAINE (1773–1811)

Adams and Liberty

[Worcester?, 1798.] Bristol 10454a. MP 48558.

As a result of the XYZ affair, Adams found himself being cheered as a veritable Washington. Even republican newspapers coined patriotic slogans, and poetry praising Adams appeared everywhere. This poem, written at the peak of the naval conflict with France, heaped praise on Adams and tried to raise the patriotic fervor of Americans. Hence the nationalistic sentiment and the repeated assertions of America's strength, virtue, valor, and liberty. The author of this very popular song, Robert Treat Paine, was a poet of

ADAMS AND LIBERTY.

YE Sons of Columbia, who bravely have fought,
 For those rights which unstain'd from your
  Sires had descended,
May you long taste the blessings your valor has
 bought,
 And your sons reap the soil, which your fathers
  defended.
  Mid the reign of mild peace,
  May our nation increase,
With the glory of Rome, and the wisdom of Greece ;

And ne'er may the sons of Columbia be slaves,
While the earth bears a plant, or the sea rolls its waves.

In a clime, whose rich vales feed the marts of the
 world,
 Whose shores are unshaken by Europe's commo-
  tion,
The trident of Commerce should never be hurl'd,
 To incense the legitimate powers of the ocean.
  But should Pirates invade,
  Though in thunder array'd,
Let your cannon declare the free charter of Trade.
 For ne'er shall, &c.

The fame of our arms, of our laws the mild sway,
 Had justly ennobled our nation in story,
Till the dark clouds of Faction obscur'd our young
 And envelop'd the sun of American glory. [day,
  But let Traitors be told,
  Who their country have sold,
And barter'd their God, for his image in gold—
 That ne'er shall, &c.

While France her huge limbs bathes recumbent in
 blood,
 And society's base threats with wide dissolution,
May Peace, like the dove who return'd from the
 flood,
 Find an ark of abode in our mild Constitution !
  But tho' Peace is our aim,
  Yet the boon we disclaim,
If bought by our Sov'reignty, Justice or Fame.
 For ne'er shall, &c.

'Tis the fire of the flint, each American warms ;
 Let Rome's haughty victors beware of collision !
Let them bring all the vassals of Europe in arms,
 We're a world by ourselves, and disdain a division !
  While, with patriot pride,
  To our laws we're ally'd,
No foe can subdue us—no faction divide.
 For ne'er shall, &c.

Our Mountains are crown'd with imperial Oak,
 Whose roots, like our liberties, ages have nou-
  rish'd
But long ere our nation submits to the yoke,
 Not a tree shall be left on the field where it
  flourish'd.
  Should invasion impend,
  Every grove would descend
From the hill-tops they shaded, our shores to defend.
 For ne'er shall, &c.

Let our Patriots destroy Anarch's pestilent worm,
 Lest our Liberty's growth should be check'd by
  corrosion ;
Then let clouds thicken round us, we heed not the
  storm ;
 Our realms fears no shock but the earth's own ex-
  plosion.
  Foes assail us in vain,
  Though their Fleets bridge the main ;
For our alters and laws with our lives we'll main-
 tain !
 And ne'er shall, &c.

Should the Tempest of War overshadow our land,
 Its bolts could ne'er rend Freedom's temple a-
  sunder ;
For, unmov'd, at its portal would Washington stand,
 And repulse with his breast the assault of the
  thunder !
  His sword from his sleep
  Of its scabbard would leap,
And conduct, with its point, every flash to the
 deep.
 For ne'er shall &c.

Let Fame to the world sound America's voice ;
 No intrigue can her sons from Government sever ;
Her pride is her Adams—his laws are her choice,
 And shall flourish, till Liberty slumber for ever ;
  Then unite heart and hand,
  Like Leonidas' band,
And swear to the God of the ocean and land,

That ne'er shall the sons of Columbia be slaves,
While the earth bear's a plant, or the sea rolls its wa

5

217. Robert Treat Paine's song praising President John Adams

Boston who was also active in the theater. 'Adams and Liberty' was sung to the tune 'To Anacreon in Heaven,' which was composed by John Stafford Smith. Francis Scott Key immortalized the tune by using it for the 'Star-Spangled Banner' in 1814.

218 WILLIAM COBBETT (1762–1835)

French Arrogance; or 'The Cat let out of the Bag'

Philadelphia, 1798. Evans 33526.

Cobbett was a journalist who wrote this pamphlet under the pen name of Peter Porcupine. An Englishman, Cobbett lived as a political refugee in New York and Philadelphia from October 1792 until June 1800. He became an unabashed Federalist and supporter of the British, and as such was one of the founders of American party journalism. Stimulated by the XYZ affair, this particular attack on the French circulated widely throughout the states. The 'Lady' referred to on the title page was Madame de Villette. The niece, adopted daughter, and reputed mistress of Voltaire, she had been linked to the American commissioners.

219

The Launch, A Federal Song

[Boston?, 1798?] Bristol 10380. MP 48501.

This song was written for the launching of the *Merrimack* on October 12, 1798. The poem described the French 'brothers' and 'lovers of liberty' of Revolutionary days as 'robbers,' praised Adams and Washington, and called for a united effort against France.

220

A Bill for the Government of the Navy of the United States

[Philadelphia, 1799.] Evans 36496.

122

The United States navy was established during Washington's administration in 1794. President Adams, however, regularized it and made it more efficient in 1798 when he created the Department of the Navy and commissioned the construction of twenty-four additional ships of war. In March 1799, Congress further strengthened the navy by passing this bill which set forth the regulations pertaining to offenses on shipboard, punishments, prize money, courts-martial, and other aspects of daily life. This revision of the existing naval code was precipitated by the fear of war with France and the general need for a responsive naval force to protect the interests and honor of the United States.

221 AMOS DOOLITTLE (1754–1832)

A New Display of the United States

Engraving, New Haven, 1803. Stauffer 509 (second state).

This portrait of John Adams surrounded by the coats of arms of the sixteen United States was engraved by Amos Doolittle. Trained as a silversmith, Doolittle taught himself the rudiments of copper engraving. As an engraver he furnished numerous portraits and illustrations for books, and engraved currency, music, diplomas, maps, and depictions of historical events. Doolittle had earlier engraved a portrait of Washington surrounded by the seals of the new nation and the states. The XYZ affair and John Adams's newfound popularity inspired Doolittle to create a similar print (first issued in 1799) in honor of the second president.

222 THOMAS JEFFERSON (1743–1826)

President Jefferson's Speech, Delivered on the Fourth of March, 1801

[Portsmouth, New Hampshire, 1801.]

Most Federalists regarded Jefferson as a cunning, scheming radical, and feared that once in power he might become a Robespierre and unleash a reign of terror. Hence this inaugural address came as a com-

President JEFFERSON's SPEECH,

DELIVERED ON THE FOURTH OF MARCH, 1801,

PREVIOUS TO HIS INAUGURATION TO THE

PRESIDENCY OF THE UNITED STATES.

FRIENDS & FELLOW CITIZENS,

CALLED upon to undertake the duties of the first Executive office of our country, I avail myself of the presence of that portion of my fellow citizens which is here assembled, to express my grateful thanks for the favor with which they have been pleased to look towards me, to declare a sincere consciousness that the task is above my talents, and that I approach it with those anxious and awful presentiments which the greatness of the charge, and the weakness of my powers so justly inspire. A rising nation, spread over a wide and fruitful land, traversing all the seas with the rich productions of their industry, engaged in commerce with nations who feel power and forget right, advancing rapidly to destinies beyond the reach of mortal eye ; when I contemplate these transcendent objects, and see the honor, the happiness, and the hopes of this beloved country committed to the issue and the auspices of this day, I shrink from the contemplation, and humble myself before the magnitude of the undertaking. Utterly indeed should I despair, did not the presence of many, whom I here see, remind me, that in the other high authorities provided by our constitution, I shall find resources of wisdom, of virtue and of zeal, on which to rely under all difficulties. To you, then, gentlemen, who are charged with the sovereign functions of legislation, and to those associated with you, I look with encouragement for that guidance and support which may enable us to steer with safety the vessel in which we are all embarked, amidst the conflicting elements of a troubled world.

During the contest of opinion thro' which we have past, the animation of discussions and of exertions has sometimes worn an aspect which might impose on strangers unused to think freely, and to speak and to write what they think ; but this being now decided by the voice of the nation, announced according to the rules of the constitution, all will of course arrange themselves under the will of the law, and unite in common efforts for the common good. All too, will bear in mind this sacred principle, that though the will of the majority is in all cases to prevail, that will, to be rightful, must be reasonable ; that the minority possess their equal rights, which equal laws must protect, and to violate would be oppression. Let us, then, fellow citizens, unite with one heart and one mind, let us restore to social intercourse that harmony and affection without which liberty, and even life itself, are but dreary things. And let us reflect that having banished from our land that religious intolerance under which mankind so long bled and suffered ; we have yet gained little, if we countenance a political intolerance, as despotic, as wicked, and capable of as bitter and bloody persecutions. During the throes and convulsions of the ancient world, during the agonizing spasms of infuriated man, seeking thro' blood and slaughter his long lost liberty, it was not wonderful that the agitation of the billows should reach even this distant and peaceful shore ; that this should be more felt and feared by some and less by others ; and should divide opinions as to measures of safety ; but every difference of opinion is not a difference of principle. We have called by different names brethren of the same principle. We are all republicans ; we are all federalists. If there be any among us who would wish to dissolve this Union, or to change its republican form, let them stand undisturbed as monuments of the safety with which error of opinion may be tolerated, where reason is left free to combat it. I know indeed that some honest men fear that a republican government cannot be strong ; that this government is not strong enough. But would the honest patriot, in the full tide of successful experiment, abandon a government which has so far kept us free and firm, on the theoretic and visionary fear, that this government, the world's best hope, may, by possibility, want energy to preserve itself ? I trust not. I believe this on the contrary, the strongest government on earth. I believe it the only one, where every man at the call of the law, would fly to the standard of the law, and would meet invasions of the public order as his own personal concern.— Sometimes it is said that man cannot be trusted with the government of himself. Can he then be trusted with the government of others? Or have we found angels in the form of kings to govern him ? Let history answer this question.

Let us then, with courage and confidence, pursue our own federal and republican principles ; our attachment to union and representative government. Kindly separated by nature and a wide ocean from the exterminating havoc of one quarter of the globe ; too high minded to endure the degradations of the others, possessing a chosen country, with room enough for our descendants to the hundredth and thousandth generation, entertaining a due sense of our equal right to the use of our own faculties, to the acquisitions of our own industry, to honor and confidence from our fellow citizens, resulting not from birth, but from our actions and their sense of them, enlightened by a benign religion, professed indeed and practised in various forms, yet all of them inculcating honesty, truth, temperance, gratitude & the love of man, acknowledging and adoring an overruling providence, which by all its dispensations proves that it delights in the happiness of man here, and his greater happiness hereafter ; with all these blessings, what more is necessary to make us a happy and a prosperous people ? Still one thing more, fellow-citizens, a wise and prudent government, which shall restrain men from injuring one another, shall leave them otherwise free to regulate their own pursuits of industry and improvement, and shall not take from the mouth of labor the bread it has earned. This is the sum of good Government ; and this is necessary to close the circle of our felicities.

About to enter, fellow citizens, on the exercise of duties which comprehend every thing dear and valuable to you, it is proper you should understand what I deem the essential principles of our government, and consequently those which ought to shape its administration. I will compress them within the narrowest compass they will bear, stating the general principle, but not all its limitations. Equal and exact justice to all men, of whatever state or persuasion, religious or political : peace, commerce & honest friendship with all nations, entangling alliances with none : the support of the state governments in all their rights, as the most competent administrations for our domestic concerns, and the surest bulwarks against anti-republican tendencies : the preservation of the general government in its whole constitutional vigor, as the sheet anchor of our peace at home, and safety abroad : a jealous care of the right of election by the people, a mild and safe corrective of abuses which are lopped by the sword of revolution where peaceable remedies are unprovided : absolute acquiescence in the decisions of the majority the vital principle of republics, from which is no appeal but to force, the vital principle and immediate parent of despotism : a well disciplined militia, our best reliance in peace, and for the first moments of war, until regulars may relieve them : the supremacy of the civil over the military authority : economy in the public expense, that labor may be lightly burthened : the honest payment of our debts and sacred preservation of the public faith : encouragement of agriculture, and of commerce as its handmaid : the diffusion of information, and arraignment of all abuses at the bar of the public reason : freedom of religion ; freedom of the press ; and freedom of person, under the protection of the Habeas Corpus : and trial by juries impartially selected. These principles form the bright constellation, which has gone before us, and guided our steps through an age of revolution and reformation. The wisdom of our sages, and blood of our heroes, have been devoted to their attainment : they should be the creed of our political faith : the text of civic instruction, the touchstone by which to try the services of those we trust ; and should we wander from them in moments of error or of alarm, let us hasten to retrace our steps, and to regain the road which alone leads to peace, liberty and safety.

I repair then, fellow citizens, to the post you have assigned me. With experience enough in subordinate offices to have seen the difficulties of this the greatest of all ; I have learnt to expect that it will rarely fall to the lot of imperfect man to retire from this station with the reputation and favor, which bring him into it. Without pretensions to that high confidence you reposed in our first and greatest revolutionary character, whose pre-eminent services had entitled him to the first place in his country's love, and destined for him the fairest page in the volume of faithful history, I ask so much confidence only as may give firmness and effect to the legal administration of your affairs. I shall often go wrong through defect of judgment. When right, I shall often be thought wrong by those whose positions will not command a view of the whole ground. I ask your indulgence for my own errors, which will never be intentional ; and your support against the errors of others, who may condemn what they would not, if seen in all its parts. The approbation implied by your suffrage, is a great consolation to me for the past ; and my future solicitude will be, to retain the good opinion of those who have bestowed it in advance, to conciliate that of others by doing them all the good in my power, and to be instrumental in the happiness and freedom of all.

Relying then on the patronage of your good will, I advance with obedience to the work, ready to retire from it whenever you become sensible how much better choices it is in your power to make. And may that infinite Power, which rules the destinies of the universe, lead our councils to what is best, and give them a favorable issue for your peace and prosperity.

THOMAS JEFFERSON.

Printed by NUTTING & WHITELOCK.

222. Thomas Jefferson's first inaugural address

forting surprise to all but the most extreme of his enemies. For those who feared Jefferson the 'atheist,' his explicit statement of faith in God was comforting. To those who feared Jefferson the 'Francophile,' he addressed a plea for 'honest friendship with all nations, entangling alliances with none.' For those who feared Jefferson the arch-partisan, he heaped great praise upon Washington and urged that the extreme partisanship of recent times be abandoned and forgotten. 'Every difference of opinion is not a difference of principle . . . ,' he said. 'We are all Republicans, we are all Federalists.'

LITERATURE

Although colonial American writers had produced hundreds of poems, no original fiction or drama had been published by 1763. The imperial crises, the Revolution, and the formation of a new nation, however, stimulated the growth of an American literature. Poets, prose writers, and dramatists emerged and tended to emphasize one theme—the uniqueness, mission, and rising glory of America. Increased study of literature in the colleges, the pride of independence, and the concept of American destiny combined to produce by 1800 a new generation of writers inspired by the promise of the new nation.

223 PHILIP MORIN FRENEAU
(1752–1832)

A Poem on the Rising Glory of America

Philadelphia, 1772. BAL 1292. Evans 12398. Gift of Donald M. Frost, 1941.

A poet, editor, and mariner of French descent, Freneau was a pioneer in the 'romantic' movement. An impassioned believer in America's destiny, as this poem, co-authored with H. H. Brackenridge, demonstrates, he wrote bitter satires about the loyalists and the 'insolent foe,' while glorifying the deeds of his fellow patriots. Because of his dedication to the American cause he won the title 'the poet of the American Revolution.' After the war he sided with the Jeffersonian Republicans and singled out Hamilton, because of his financial program, as America's chief enemy. He was probably the most significant poet in America before William Cullen Bryant.

224 MERCY OTIS WARREN
(1728–1814)

The Group

Boston, 1775. Evans 15213.

The sister of James Otis and the wife of James Warren, Mercy Otis Warren was an historian, poet, and dramatist. She possessed an uncommon talent for literature and politics, and became closely associated with those high in the Revolutionary councils of Massachusetts. As a result, she became in a manner the poet laureate and later the historical apologist for the patriot cause. Two political satires, *The Adulateur* (1773) and this play, are deserving of particular mention. Both works demonstrate vast historical knowledge, a penetrating analysis of contemporary political figures, and a fervent American patriotism. She also was an articulate advocate of women's rights and communicated her feelings on the subject to Samuel Adams, James Winthrop, John Dickinson, Thomas Jefferson, Elbridge Gerry, and Henry Knox.

225 JOHN TRUMBULL (1750–1831)

M'Fingal: A Modern Epic Poem

Philadelphia, 1775. Evans 14528.

Trumbull was a poet, jurist, and patriot, who wrote *M'Fingal* at the suggestion of some leading members of the first Congress. After the war, he divided the poem into two cantos and wrote two additional ones.

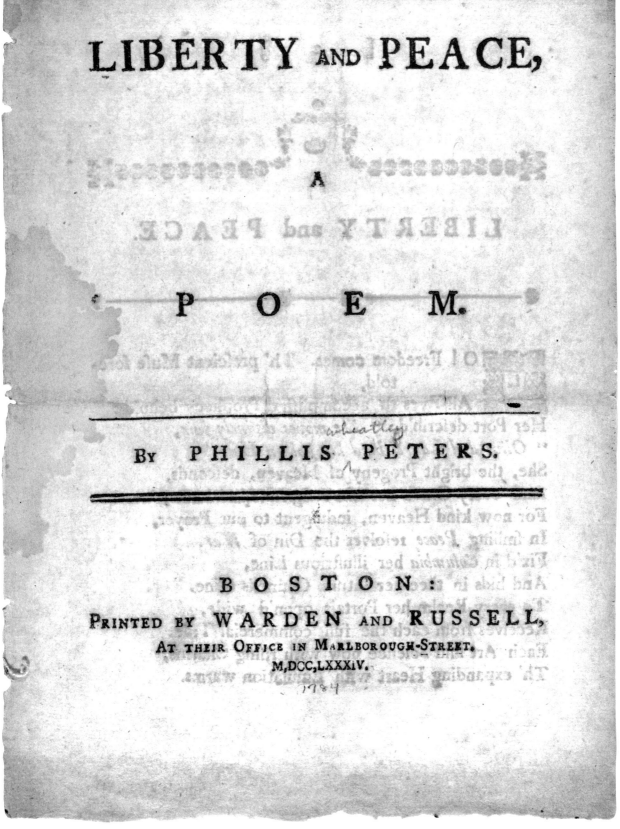

LIBERTY AND PEACE,

A

POEM.

By PHILLIS PETERS.

BOSTON:

Printed by WARDEN and RUSSELL,

At their Office in Marlborough-Street.

M,DCC,LXXXIV.

1784

226. Phillis Wheatley's poem on liberty and peace

The framework of the poem is a loosely unified narrative of the misfortunes of the Tory squire M'Fingal; but the poem virtually constitutes a comprehensive review of the blunders and cowardice of the British leaders throughout the Revolution. In addition to its patriotic overtones, this poem was invested with literary qualities which received their fullest recognition after the war. The merits of *M'Fingal* gave Trumbull the position of literary leader of the 'Hartford Wits' during the 1780s and '90s.

226 PHILLIS WHEATLEY (1753–1784)

Liberty and Peace, A Poem

Boston, 1784. Evans 18727.

Born in Africa, Phillis Wheatley was brought to America at the age of eight and sold to John Wheatley of Boston. She learned English rapidly and also became fascinated by Greek mythology, Greek and Roman history, and the contemporary English poets. She began writing verse when she was thirteen and had her first book of poems published in 1773. Freed in 1778, she married John Peters, a free black. Despite her period of bondage, this poem celebrated America's liberty and destiny.

227 TIMOTHY DWIGHT (1752–1817)

The Conquest of Canaan

Hartford, 1785. BAL 5040. Evans 18996.

Dwight was a Congregational minister who served as president of Yale College from 1795 to 1817. *The Conquest of Canaan,* the first epic poem to appear in America, consists of eleven books in rhymed pentameters, and was an audacious attempt to give the New World an epic such as the *Iliad* or the *Aeneid.*

228 JOEL BARLOW (1754–1812)

The Vision of Columbus; A Poem in Nine Books

Hartford, 1787. BAL 865. Evans 20220.

Barlow, a poet and diplomat, was destined by temperament and circumstances to become one of the most liberal thinkers of his age. He first published prose and poetry at a very early age. He always had the ambition to write the 'great poem,' the vast epic of America. In 1787 appeared the proof of his literary dreams, *The Vision of Columbus,* which had taken eight years to write. Despite obvious debts to Milton and stretches of wretched verse, it was well received and made Barlow famous. His countrymen found his grandiose couplets on the discovery, settlement, and majestic future of America irresistible.

229

Ode for the 23d of October, 1792

No place, [1792]. Evans 24642.

This ode captures the surging spirit of American nationalism in the 1790s. It expresses the familiar concept of a corrupt Europe looking to America for guidance and asserts that God had a special mission for America. The poem emphasizes the westward movement of liberty and the abundance of 'Columbia's favored soil.'

230 HUGH HENRY BRACKENRIDGE (1748–1816)

The Death of General Montgomery

Norwich, Connecticut, 1777. BAL 1295. Evans 15250. Gift of Thomas Wallcut, 1834.

231 HUGH HENRY BRACKENRIDGE (1748–1816)

Modern Chivalry: Containing the Adventures of Captain John Farrago, and Teague Oregan, His Servant

Part I, 4 vols. Philadelphia, 1792–1797. BAL 1300–1301, 1304. Evans 24142.

Brackenridge was born in Scotland, and migrated to America in 1753. The classmate of Philip Freneau and

ODE

FOR THE 23ᴰ OF OCTOBER, 1792.

1 WHEN form'd by GOD's creating Hand,
    This beauteous fabrick first appear'd;
Eternal Wisdom gave command,
    All Nature with attention heard.

2 " Here, *Ocean*, roll thy swelling tide;
    " Here spread thy vast Atlantic main;
" From European eyes to hide
    " That Western World, which bounds thy reign."

3 Whilst *Ocean* kept his sacred charge,
    And fair Columbia lay conceal'd;
Through Europe, *Discord* roam'd at large,
    Till *War* had crimson'd every field.

4 Black *Superstition*'s dismal night
    Extinguish'd *Reason*'s golden ray;
And *Science*, driven from the light,
    Beneath monastic rubbish lay.

5 The *Crown* and *Mitre*, close ally'd,
    Trampled whole nations to the dust;
Whilst FREEDOM, wandering far and wide,
    With pure RELIGION, both were lost.

6 Then, guided by th' Almighty Hand,
    COLUMBUS spread his daring sail;
Ocean receiv'd a new command,
    And *Zephyrs* breath'd a gentle gale.

7 The Western World appear'd to view,
    Her friendly arms extended wide;
Then FREEDOM o'er th' Atlantic flew,
    With pure RELIGION by her side.

8 Tyrants with mortal hate pursu'd;
    In vain their forces they employ;
In vain the Serpent pours his flood,
    Those heaven-born Exiles to destroy.

9 " No weapon form'd against my flock
    " Shall prosper," saith th' Almighty Lord;
" Their proudest threatnings thou shalt mock,
    " For I will be thy shield and sword.

10 " Sweet peace and heav'nly truth shall shine
    " On fair Columbia's happy ground;
" There FREEDOM and RELIGION join,
    " And spread their influence all around."

CHORUS.

11 Hail! GREAT COLUMBIA! favour'd soil;
Thy fields with plenty crown thy toil;
Thy shore, the seat of growing wealth;
Thy clime the source of balmy health.

12 From thee proceeds the virtuous plan,
To vindicate the *Rights of Man*.
Thy fame shall spread from pole to pole,
Whilst everlasting ages roll.

229. Ode celebrating America's special mission

James Madison at Princeton, he became devoted to literature and political issues. He helped Freneau write *The Rising Glory of America* in 1771, and he openly supported American resistance. During the Revolution, Brackenridge contributed patriotic writings to the cause and served as chaplain. During this time he wrote *The Battle of Bunker's Hill* (1776) and *The Death of General Montgomery* (1777), the former depicting the superior fighting spirit of the Americans, and the latter foretelling the future greatness of the American Union. In 1781 Brackenridge moved to Pittsburgh where he set up the first newspaper and the first bookstore as well as the Pittsburgh Academy. During this time he wrote his most important work, *Modern Chivalry*, a picaresque novel which lampooned the social and political ambitions of the uneducated and incapable.

232   JEREMY BELKNAP (1744–1798)

The Foresters, An American Tale

Boston, 1792. BAL 929. Evans 24086. Gift of the Estate of Lawrence S. Mayo, 1949.

Belknap was a Congregational clergyman who wrote the very well received *History of New Hampshire*. In 1787 he wrote this humorous allegory which described the origin, rise, and inevitable destiny of the British colonies in North America. It appeared serially in *The Columbian Magazine*, and later the chapters were collected in this small book. Belknap was also one of the founders of the Massachusetts Historical Society, the first historical society in the nation.

233   SAMUEL HARRIS (1783–1810)

Portrait of Jeremy Belknap (1744–1798)

Red chalk drawing, ca. 1805. Bequest of William Bentley, 1819.

William Bentley probably commissioned Samuel Harris, a portrait draftsman and engraver in Boston, to make this drawing of Belknap because of the lat-

ter's impressive *History of New Hampshire*, published in three volumes from 1784 to 1792. In many ways, it was comparable to Hutchinson's *History of the Colony of Massachusetts-Bay* (1764–1767), except that it covered the period to 1790 and included a treatise on the natural history of the state. Belknap also compiled *American Biography* (1794–1798), which contained biographical sketches of people important in the history of America.

234   WILLIAM HILL BROWN (1766–1793)

The Power of Sympathy: or The Triumph of Nature

2 vols. Boston, 1789. BAL 1518. Evans 21979.

Brown's plays, though of minor significance as literature, demonstrated the obsession American writers had with virtue. Dedicated to the women of America, this play was designed to caution young ladies against the paths of wickedness and to remind them of the important role they all had in America's future greatness. This was Isaiah Thomas's own copy, specially bound.

235   ROYALL TYLER (1757–1826)

The Contrast

Philadelphia, 1790. Evans 22948.

A playwright, novelist, and jurist, Tyler was also interested in painting and politics. While in New York in 1787, he was so inspired by the theater that he wrote *The Contrast,* the second play and the first comedy penned by a native American and produced by a professional company. It was a very successful satire of British manners and those who affected a British 'style.' His character Brother Jonathan became one of the first fictional characters to symbolize the naive, innocent, shrewd, intelligent, virtuous, and brave nature of 'the' American.

BUNKER-HILL;

OR THE

DEATH OF GENERAL WARREN:

AN

HISTORIC TRAGEDY.

IN

FIVE ACTS.

BY JOHN BURK,

LATE OF TRINITY COLLEGE, DUBLIN.

AS PLAYED AT THE THEATRES IN AMERICA, FOR
FOURTEEN NIGHTS, WITH UNBOUNDED
APPLAUSE.

NEW-YORK: PRINTED BY T. GREENLEAF.

M,DCC,XCVII.

238. John Daly Burk's play about the Battle of Bunker Hill

236

Theatre, Frederick-Town. By Mr. M'Grath's Company of Comedians . . . The Celebrated Comedy of . . . The Contrast

Fredericktown, Maryland, [1791]. Bristol 7703. MP 46169.

This unique advertisement for Royall Tyler's play *The Contrast* emphasizes the American origin of the play ('written by a Citizen of the United States') and its popularity.

237 SUSANNA HASWELL ROWSON (1762–1824)

Slaves in Algiers

Philadelphia, 1794. Evans 27655. Gift of Matt B. Jones, 1936.

Mrs. Rowson was a novelist, playwright, actress, and educator. Born in England, she emigrated to Massachusetts when she was five, and the stormy sea passage was recounted in her novel *Rebecca*. Better known for her works of fiction, especially *Charlotte, a Tale of Truth*, which became the chief American fictional 'best seller' before *Uncle Tom's Cabin*, she wrote *Slaves in Algiers* for a Philadelphia company of actors. Her plays and her verse address 'The Standard of Liberty' demonstrated her view of the 'rising glory' of America, and gained her an ardent following.

238 JOHN DALY BURK (1775–1808)

Bunker-Hill; or the Death of General Warren

A dramatist born in Ireland, Burk came to America in 1796 as a political refugee. He settled in Boston, started a newspaper which failed, and then went to New York where he repeated this experience. He finally settled in Virginia and was killed in a duel. Though he wrote a history of Ireland and a four-volume *History of Virginia*, it was as a playwright that he is best known. He was among the earliest to put an American battle scene on the stage, in *Bunker-Hill*, which was first produced in 1797 in New York. This play, which celebrated American courage, virtue, and liberty, remained popular on such holidays as the Fourth of July for almost fifty years.

239 WILLIAM DUNLAP (1766–1839)

The Father; or, American Shandy-ism

New York, 1789. BAL 4974. Evans 21805.

240 WILLIAM DUNLAP (1766–1839)

Andre; a Tragedy

New York, 1798. BAL 4980. Evans 33652.

Dunlap was a playwright, theatrical manager, historian, and painter. Among those who sat for one of his canvasses were George and Martha Washington. He deserted painting for the stage, however, and his second play, *The Father*, met with sufficient success to focus his ambition upon the theater. He also began to write narrative poems of some length, and was the first in this country to write gothic plays such as *Fontainville Abbey* (1795) and *Ribbemont: or, the Feudal Baron* (1796). His plays were far superior to most others of his time, and *The Father* and *Andre* are two of the most memorable American plays of the eighteenth century.

American architecture after the Revolution was greatly stimulated by the influx of foreign-born architects who sought shelter in the United States from the disorders in their native lands. These men combined their considerable talents and insights with those of American-born architects and created the Federal style of American architecture. This blend of classical elements with traditional Georgian and colonial styles provided a new architectural mode which Americans used in public buildings, banks, homes, churches, and educational institutions.

Though not a contributor to the Federal style, Asher Benjamin also had a significant impact on American architecture, for he was the first American to compile and publish a handbook for the guidance of carpenters and house builders. Another significant figure was Thomas Jefferson, who dreamed not of teaching carpenters the rudiments of building, but of charting the course of American civil architecture. He hoped his designs would be models for his countrymen to study and imitate for centuries.

241 PIERRE CHARLES L'ENFANT (1754-1825)

View of the Federal Edifice in New York

Engraving, *Columbian Magazine*, Philadelphia, 1789.

In 1789 the citizens of New York renovated their city hall for use as the new nation's capitol and for Washington's inauguration. Pierre L'Enfant designed the exterior and interior renovations, which were largely decorative. The most significant alterations were the additions of the eagle on the pediment, the stars between the metopes, and the olive branches and arrows over the windows. Washington was inaugurated on the balcony of the building, which combines a variety of colonial and classical elements, central features of the Federal style.

242 BENJAMIN HENRY LATROBE (1764-1820)

Centre Square Philada. [Pump House]

Engraving, *The Portfolio*, Philadelphia, 1812.

Latrobe, an architect and engineer, was born in England and studied under Samuel Pepys Cockerell, a pioneer of the Greek revival. He emigrated to America in 1796 and immediately contributed to the Federal style of architecture by infusing classic revivalism with the traditional Georgian and colonial modes of American architecture. Latrobe was the engineer of the Philadelphia waterworks, which included the Pump House, designed in 1800. The core of this structure was a cylindrical mass which rose through the whole height of the building. Contained within its walls beneath its domed top was the water tank. At the bottom was a square structure which housed the pumping machinery and offices. The composition of masses, therefore, was a bold piling of geometric shapes. Latrobe used the same stark geometrical forms in his designs for the Bank of Pennsylvania (1798-1801).

243 CHARLES BULFINCH (1763-1844)

An East View of the Meeting House in Hollis St, Boston

Columbian Magazine, Philadelphia, 1788. Stauffer 3341.

Bulfinch learned much of his art as an architect while touring England and the Continent in 1785-1787. His first design, submitted in November 1787 soon after his return to Boston from abroad, had been for a new state house, but this project remained in abeyance for a time. In 1788 the Hollis Street Church was built

THE

COUNTRY BUILDER's

ASSISTANT:

—CONTAINING—

A COLLECTION OF NEW DESIGNS OF

CARPENTRY AND ARCHITECTURE,

Which will be particularly useful, to Country Workmen in general.

ILLUSTRATED WITH NEW AND USEFUL DESIGNS OF

Frontispieces, Chimney Pieces, &c. Tuscan, Doric, Ionic, and Corinthian
Orders, with their Bases, Capitals, and Entablatures : Architraves for Doors,
Windows, and Chimneys : Cornices, Base, and Surbase Mouldings for
Rooms : Doors, and Sashes, with their Mouldings : The construction of Stairs,
with their Ramp and Twist Rails : Plan, Elevation, and one Section of a
Meetinghouse, with the Pulpit at large : Plans and Elevations of Houses :
The best Method of finding the length, and backing of Hip Rafters : Also,
the tracing of Groins, Angle Brackets, Circular Soffits in Circular Walls, &c.

CORRECTLY ENGRAVED ON THIRTY COPPER PLATES ;
WITH A PRINTED EXPLANATION TO EACH.

———

BY ASHER BENJAMIN.

━━━━━━━━━━━━━━━━

PRINTED AT GREENFIELD, (MASSACHUSETTS)
BY THOMAS DICKMAN.

M,DCC,XCVII.

247. Asher Benjamin's builder's guide for American craftsmen

from his plans, and was followed by designs for churches at Taunton and Pittsfield. He also designed the State House at Hartford (1792), the Boston Theatre (1793), the Massachusetts State House, and many domestic dwellings. He was one of the foremost contributors to an American Federal Style of architecture.

244 CHARLES BULFINCH (1763–1844)

Worcester County Court House

Wash drawing by Jeremiah Stiles, 1804.

This drawing of the nineteenth-century Worcester County Court House was made by Jeremiah Stiles (1771–1826) from the original elevation (1801) of Charles Bulfinch. The agent for the court house project was Isaiah Thomas. The building was completed in 1803 and demolished in 1898. Its outstanding feature was a substantial glazed cupola bearing a statue of Justice.

245 SAMUEL McINTIRE (1757–1811)

[Benjamin Pickman House, Salem, Massachusetts], 1786

Lithograph, Boston, ca. 1825.

McIntire was a wood-carver and architect from Massachusetts who single-handedly created an architectural style for the town of Salem. This house, built in 1764 for Benjamin Pickman, was extensively remodelled by McIntire during the 1780s. The owner, Elias Hasket Derby, commissioned McIntire to add the Roman Revival porch, the corner pilasters on the west facade, and various other items of classical trim and ornamentation which gave the house its Federal-style appearance.

The lithograph was drawn by Mary Jane Derby (1807–1892), an amateur artist. Her father, John Derby, owned the house for many years after 1800.

246 SAMUEL BLODGETT, JR. (1757–1814)

The Bank of the United States of America

Engraving, [London?, ca. 1800].

Blodgett was a merchant and economist from New Hampshire. Although not a professional architect, he designed the building for the first Bank of the United States. The first important building in the United States to be made of marble extensively, it was the physical embodiment of the federal monetary system successfully promoted by Alexander Hamilton. Derived from the Royal Exchange in Dublin, the building featured a giant order of pilasters and a columned portico. It was one of the earliest buildings of the Neoclassical revival.

247 ASHER BENJAMIN (1773–1845)

The Country Builder's Assistant

Greenfield, Massachusetts, 1797.

Benjamin was an architect whose renown was spread by his various handbooks. Through his books, such as this one, architectural details and designs were broadcast throughout New England, as English ideas had been broadcast by English books in colonial times. There is scarcely a village in which some moulding profiles, cornice details, church spire, or farmhouse designs do not reflect his influence. This was not the first book on architecture printed in America, but it was the first original American treatise. So great was the need for builders' guides designed for American needs that this and the six other handbooks bearing Benjamin's name were published in more than forty editions.

248 THOMAS JEFFERSON (1743–1826)

University of Virginia, Charlottesville

Engraving, London, 1831.

249 THOMAS JEFFERSON (1743–1826)

Capitol of Virginia, Richmond

Engraving, London, 1831.

Often called 'the father of our national architecture,' Jefferson designed numerous public buildings in addition to his own palatial country residence, Monticello. For example, he did the Virginia State Capitol (1785), pictured here in an 1831 English engraving of a drawing by William Goodacre of New York City. Jefferson also designed the University of Virginia (1817–1826), depicted here in another 1831 engraving of William Goodacre's drawing. In addition, Jefferson designed, wholly or in part, numerous Virginia houses incorporating many classical elements. Indeed, he probably did more than any other man to stimulate a classical revival in America.

MUSIC

Musical life in colonial America focused on the performance rather than on the composition of music. The early New England colonists viewed the singing of psalms as an integral part of their lives. But by the early eighteenth century the singing of psalms had deteriorated to such an extent that in the 1720s ministers began to call for a musical reform. Singing schools and masters emerged to fill the need and soon singing school instruction became popular throughout the colonies for both sacred and secular music. The earliest American composers, such as William Billings, developed from this movement to create a distinctive musical style. A generation of Yankee tunesmiths emerged during and after the Revolution to provide stirring sacred and secular music.

Concert music and operas of European origin were frequently performed in the growing cities of colonial America. On a less sophisticated level was the singing of popular songs and ballads. The Revolution and the Federal period produced a large amount of military music, including patriotic songs and marches, as well as instrumental and vocal music.

---

250 WILLIAM BILLINGS (1746–1800)

The New-England Psalm-Singer: or American Chorister

Boston, 1770. Evans 11572.

251 WILLIAM BILLINGS (1746–1800)

The Continental Harmony

Boston, 1794. Evans 26673.

Billings had originally been a tanner and was wholly untutored in music. He was a music enthusiast, however, and possessed enough talent to begin composing at an early age. Billings lived at a time when the number of tunes was very limited. Church choirs were eager for something new. He was aware of this situation, and he soon abandoned his trade to become a singing teacher and trainer of choirs. He wrote this book, the first published volume of American-composed music, to aid in his work. As a result, his influence became deep and far-reaching. He also composed several other books of music, including *The Continental Harmony*, which, as is apparent from the title, he hoped would be useful throughout the nation.

252 JACOB KIMBALL (1761–1826)

The Rural Harmony

Boston, 1793. Evans 25695.

Kimball, who had been a drummer in the American Revolution, turned to composing and teaching music during the 1780s. He taught in several towns throughout New England. This book is typical of many such collections which tended to provide Americans with a common bond of music.

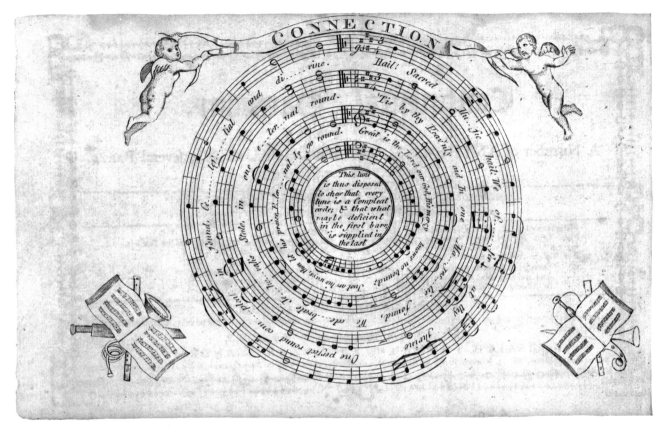

251. William Billings's tune book, *The Continental Harmony*

253 ANDREW LAW (1745-1821)

The Art of Singing

Cheshire, Connecticut, 1794. Evans 27204.

Law was a composer, compiler, and pioneer teacher of sacred music. By the time he was nineteen years old, he had compiled *A Select Number of Plain Tunes Adapted to Congregational Worship*. By 1790 he had issued at least six books of hymns or tunes, many of which were his own compositions. This book, first published in 1792, was made up of three previous works, *The Musical Primer*, the *Christian Harmony*, and *The Musical Magazine*. The publication of this and other music books helped stimulate the growth of native American music. As a singing-master, Law travelled not only throughout New England but also in New York, New Jersey, Pennsylvania, Maryland, and the Carolinas.

254 BENJAMIN CARR (1768-1831)

The Archers, or Mountaineers of Switzerland

New York, 1796. Evans 30369.

The Archers, sometimes called the first American opera, had its premiere performance on April 18, 1796. The music was composed by Benjamin Carr, an organist, singer, and publisher from England, who had emigrated to New York in 1793. He was a favorite of the American public as a ballad singer and tried the operatic stage with some success in 1794-1795. His career as concert manager, composer, and publisher, however, was of far greater importance.

William Dunlap (1766-1839), who wrote the libretto to this opera, was a man of unusual versatility who touched the American cultural life of his day at

many points. *The Archers* was adapted from a dramatic piece, *Helvetic Liberty*.

255 JAMES HEWITT (1770-1827)

The Federal Constitution and Liberty for Ever

New York, [1798]. Sonneck-Upton, p. 138.

Born in England, Hewitt emigrated to the United States in 1792 and began a career as musician, composer, teacher, and music publisher. He managed excellent subscription concerts in New York during the 1790s and was active as the orchestra leader of the Old American Company. During this period he composed several patriotic songs such as this one. The lyricist was William Milns (1761-1801), another transplanted Englishman, who became a well-known author, bookseller, and teacher in New York City from 1795 to 1800. That two transplanted Englishmen produced this song of praise to Adams, the American Constitution, and principles of liberty gives testimony to the fervent patriotism of the era.

256 TIMOTHY SWAN (1758-1842)

New England Harmony

Northampton, Massachusettes, 1801. Shaw 1378.

Swan, who was born in Worcester, had a limited musical education but nevertheless managed to compose a large number of hymns and secular songs. He began composing at the age of seventeen while working as a hatter. He knew what pleased the people, for his music, whether religious or secular, became very popular. One of his best-known patriotic songs, a stirring anthem to George Washington, appears on pages 12-13 of this book.

PAINTING

After the Revolution Americans felt pride in their newly won independence and their own individual accomplishments. Accordingly, in the 1780s and '90s many people of a broad social spectrum, hired portrait painters. And there was a well-trained and productive group of American artists from which to choose. Many of these new painters had been trained and encouraged by Copley, West, Peale, Stuart, and Trumbull, America's first masters. But unlike some of their mentors, who chose to paint in Europe, this new generation of artists for the most part found America to be a fertile environment for their growth and development.

Thus by 1800, though American art eschewed the grace of the French, the grandeur of the Italian, and the aristocratic tone of the English Rococo painting, it had its own energy and integrity. The people of America were a new and vibrant people, and their art not only reflected their images, but captured their strong, earnest, independent, and bourgeois spirit as well.

257 MATHER BROWN (1761–1831)

Self-portrait

Oil on canvas. Gift of Mrs. Frederick L. Gay, 1923.

258 MATHER BROWN (1761–1831)

Portrait of Mather Byles Junior (1735–1814)

Oil on canvas, 1784. Gift of Mrs. Frederick L. Gay, 1923.

Brown was an itinerant portrait painter and wine merchant from Massachusetts who studied under Benjamin West in England and chose to live his adult life there. He exhibited over a hundred portraits in London galleries, including the portrait of Byles and the self-portrait.

259 WINTHROP CHANDLER (1747–1790)

Self-portrait

Oil on canvas. Gift of Mrs. Arthur J. Hillman, 1925.

Chandler was a portrait and landscape painter from Connecticut, who was especially sought after for his portraiture in the 1770s and '80s. He studied art in Boston, possibly under Copley. Before his untimely death he had painted many of New England's most prominent citizens.

260 MATTHEW PRATT (1734–1805)

Portrait of John Bush (1755–1816)

Oil on canvas, ca. 1785. Gift of Mrs. Maria Platt Chaffin, 1896.

261 MATTHEW PRATT (1734–1805)

Portrait of Charity Platt Bush (1761–1788)

Oil on canvas, ca. 1785. Gift of Mrs. Maria Platt Chaffin, 1896.

Pratt served his apprenticeship with his uncle, James Claypoole, a limner and general painter. He began his career as a portrait painter in 1758 in Philadelphia, and then, like Mather Brown, studied under Benjamin West in London. In the 1780s and '90s Pratt found his talents much in demand by Americans such as John Bush, a broker and cattle dealer, who wanted his wife's images preserved for his descendants.

264. John Johnston's portrait of Samuel Dexter

262 CHRISTIAN GULLAGER
(1762–1826)

Portrait of David West, Jr. (1790–1825)

Oil on canvas, 1790s. Bequest of Henry W. Cunningham, 1931.

263 CHRISTIAN GULLAGER
(1762–1826)

Portrait of Abigail Leonard West (1796–1879)

Oil on canvas, 1790s. Bequest of Henry W. Cunningham, 1931.

These portraits of David and Abigail West's children were done by Christian Gullager, a Danish immigrant who also did the likeness of Col. John May [162]. He made his living, however, by painting the portraits of average Americans who had been successful enough to afford to hire Gullager.

264 JOHN JOHNSTON (1753–1818)

Portrait of Samuel Dexter (1726–1810)

Oil on canvas, 1792. Gift of Mrs. Artemus Ward Lamson, 1936.

Johnston was another of those portrait painters of the 1780s and '90s who kept busy doing the portraits of the rising American middle class. He had learned his skills in his father's shop in Boston where Thomas Johnston sold colors, made charts, painted coats of arms, and engraved portraits and music plates. Later he fought in the Revolution and reached the rank of major. This portrait depicts Samuel Dexter of Dedham, who at various times in his life was a member of the Governor's Council, the General Court, and the Provincial Congress of Massachusetts and served as a town clerk and selectman.

LIST OF AUTHORITIES CITED

ADAMS
Thomas R. Adams. American Independence: The Growth of an Idea. Providence: Brown University Press, 1965.

BAL
Jacob Blanck. Bibliography of American Literature. 6 vols. to date, New Haven: Yale University Press, 1955–.

BRISTOL
Roger P. Bristol. Supplement to Charles Evans' American Bibliography. Charlottesville: University Press of Virginia, 1970.

EVANS
Charles Evans. American Bibliography. 14 vols., Chicago and Worcester, 1903–1959.

FIELDING
Mantle Fielding. American Engravers upon Copper and Steel. Philadelphia, 1917.

MP
Early American Imprints 1639–1800. Edited by the American Antiquarian Society. New York: Readex Microprint Corporation.
Clifford K. Shipton and James E. Mooney. National Index of American Imprints Through 1800: The Short-Title Evans, 2 vols., [Worcester]: American Antiquarian Society and Barre Publishers, 1969.

NEBENZAHL
Kenneth Nebenzahl. A Bibliography of Printed Battle Plans of the American Revolution 1775–1795. Chicago & London: University of Chicago Press, 1975.

SHAW
Ralph R. Shaw and Richard H. Shoemaker. American Bibliography: A Preliminary Checklist. 19 vols., New York: The Scarecrow Press, 1958–1963.

SONNECK-UPTON
Oscar George Theodore Sonneck and William Treat Upton. A Bibliography of Early Secular American Music. [Washington]: The Library of Congress, 1945.

STAUFFER
David McNeely Stauffer. American Engravers upon Copper and Steel. 2 vols., New York: The Grolier Club, 1907.

WHEAT & BRUN
James Clements Wheat and Christian F. Brun. Maps and Charts Published in America Before 1800: A Bibliography. New Haven and London: Yale University Press, 1969.

DATE DUE